Left Without a

HANDKERCHIEF

With thanks to Michael Roden, without whose generous support this book would not have been written.

Left Without a
HANDKERCHIEF

ROBERT O'BYRNE

THE LILLIPUT PRESS

First published 2022 by

THE LILLIPUT PRESS
62–63 Arbour Hill
Dublin 7, Ireland
www.lilliputpress.ie

A CIP record for this publication is available from The British
Library.

10 9 8 7 6 5 4 3 2

ISBN 978 1 84351 8181

The Lilliput Press gratefully acknowledges the financial support
of the Arts Council/An Chomhairle Ealaíon and the Howth
Group.

Set in 11.5pt on 17pt Sabon LT Pro by Niall McCormack.
Printed in Dublin by SprintPrint

Contents

Illustrations between pages 106 and 107.

Introduction

ON THE AFTERNOON of 10 January 1923 Louise Bagwell wrote a short letter to her mother-in-law Harriet describing what had taken place during the previous night. At around 12.30 am a large group of men had arrived at Marlfield, County Tipperary, which had been home to the Bagwell family for some 230 years, and informed the house's occupants they had ten minutes to dress and gather up whatever items they could. Meanwhile, the intruders sprinkled petrol around the ground-floor rooms and applied a match. 'Then,' Louise Bagwell explained, 'for an hour we had to stand and watch the darling old home burn.' Only when the fire had done sufficient damage to the building did the men depart: afterwards its chatelaine discovered they had taken her bag and coat with them. Everything had been lost, she lamented, all the family's possessions going back generations, leaving them with little other than the clothes they had hastily donned: 'We hadn't even a handkerchief.'

When it came to Irish country house burnings during these years, the Bagwells' circumstances were not unusual. What happened to them was standard procedure. Typically, a large group of men, most often masked, would arrive in the early hours of the morning at the door of a property demanding entry and, if this was not forthcoming, would break some windows to gain access. Whoever was in residence would be given a short period, anything from ten minutes to half an hour, to get dressed and get out. While they were pulling on clothes and, in their half-awake state, trying to decide what ought to be saved, petrol was liberally spread over carpets and furniture before being set alight. To stop them trying to extinguish the flames or seeking help, the owners would be kept at gunpoint until the fire had taken a firm hold of the building.

The Bagwells were especially vulnerable since Louise's husband John was a senator and during the Civil War opponents of the Anglo-Irish Treaty made a policy of attacking the homes of Seanad Éireann members in the hope of weakening the Free State government. In total, the homes of thirty-seven senators were burned over the course of the Civil War. Only a month before Marlfield was gutted by fire, on 8 December 1922, Liam Lynch, IRA Chief of Staff, had issued an order that 'all Free State supporters are traitors and deserve the latter's stark fate, therefore their houses must be destroyed at once'. When raiders arrived at Palmerstown, County Kildare in late January 1923, they asked the house's owner, the Earl of Mayo, whether he was a Free State senator. Confirming this was the case, he asked whether he was going to be shot. 'No, my lord,' came the response, 'we are not going to shoot you, but we have our orders to burn the building.'

This is one reason why many more country houses were burnt during the Civil War than during the earlier War of Independence. It was part of a specific policy, and could be put into effect not least because the new Free State's Civic Guards (replaced in August 1923 by the Garda Síochána) were still struggling to take over duties previously held by the Royal Irish Constabulary (RIC). Furthermore, in the spring of 1920 during the earlier War of Independence, the IRA adopted a deliberate policy of attacking and burning local Royal Irish Constabulary stations, leaving large swathes of rural Ireland, where country houses were located, without the immediate presence of law enforcers. Hence the number of such properties that were burnt after that date rose substantially. At a time when the telephone service scarcely existed and motorized transport was rare, the nearest police station might be a roofless ruin, and the next one ten or fifteen miles away. Furthermore, when there were so many other demands on officialdom, during both the War of Independence and the Civil War, assistance for country houses and their owners was not necessarily considered a priority.

Nevertheless, the number of these buildings that suffered violent attack during both tumultuous periods was smaller than used to be thought: it is estimated the figure was around 76 over the course of the War of Independence and 199 in the Civil War. In other words, the combined total was less than 300. As Mark Bence-Jones noted in his guide to Irish country houses (1978), many more of the 2000 such buildings that stood before the outbreak of the First World War would be lost through abandonment or demolition over the middle decades of the last century than went up in flames in the first half of the 1920s. On the other hand, that slow drip of destruction made less of an impression on the public imagination than did the earlier arson attacks. It also caused much less dread among owners, who at least could choose if and when to sell the family home and move elsewhere. During the War of Independence and Civil War, on the other hand, even if fewer of them experienced an actual attack, the fear that their home might be next meant some owners simply packed up and left. And those who remained in residence did so with the constant fear that one night soon they would hear the dreaded hammering at the door. Lady Mabel Annesley would recall how every night in Castlewellan, she would sit 'in tweed skirt and thick shoes, with valuables packed in suitcases ready to throw out of the window' should the house be attacked. Similarly, *Seventy Years Young*, the vivid memoirs of Elizabeth, Countess of Fingall, concludes with a description of her husband and herself sitting in his study, she in a fur coat with a jewel case on her knees, waiting for an attack on Killeen Castle that had been threatened: in the event, it never happened, and the house survived until gutted by arsonists in 1981.

Some houses, although threatened with attack, were not destroyed. One night a group of men appeared at the front door of Glin Castle, County Limerick and announced their intention to burn down the place. FitzJohn Lloyd FitzGerald, 27th Knight of Glin who in consequence of a stroke some years earlier was confined to a wheelchair, met them and declared, 'Well you will have to burn me in it, boys.' Checked in their resolve, the men retreated to the village pub where, it was said, the locals got them so drunk they were unable to return and finish their intended task. On the other side of the country, Curraghmore, County Waterford, ancestral home of the de la Poer Beresfords, Marquesses of Waterford, survived supposedly because on the night it was due to be burnt, there was a full moon behind the cross that rises with the stag of St Hubert on the roof, and the putative attackers, taking this as a sign from on high that they should do nothing, quietly slipped away.

Despite the violence of their actions the raiders were not, as a rule, aggressive, although there were a few exceptions. In mid-April 1921, for example, Sir Arthur Vicars, former Ulster King of Arms, was taken from Kilmorna House, County Kerry where he lived and was shot dead in front of his wife, the property then being set alight: the ostensible reason for this murder was that Vicars had been passing information about local IRA activity to the British army. Such incidents were fortunately rare. Daisy Fingall's memoirs recount that when Lismullin, County Meath, home of her neighbour Sir John Dillon, was burnt in April 1923, the group of men responsible apologized for what they were about to do, and helped to remove some of the better pictures and furniture from the building before setting it alight. House owners were frequently shown courtesy. The Earl of Mayo recalled that the men who burned down Palmerstown were 'excessively polite'. When Ballyrankin, County Wexford was burnt in July 1921, its owners Walter and Agnes Skrine (parents of future novelist Molly Keane), after being held at gunpoint in the study, were then taken outside and offered armchairs in which to sit while their home was destroyed. The offer was declined, Walter Skrine putting up such a struggle to stop his property being burned that one of the raiders apologetically warned, 'Please steady yourself, Captain, or we will have to shoot you.' To which came the reply, 'I would rather be shot in Ireland than live in England.'

Certain parts of the country experienced more burnings than others. Ulster, with its substantial unionist population, came off lightest, although a number of houses were destroyed in what are now the border counties of Monaghan and Cavan. The further south, the greater likelihood of country houses being attacked. Munster experienced the greatest quantity of burnings, especially County Cork as well as counties Tipperary, Wexford and Waterford. Since the relatively poor quality of land in the west of Ireland meant there were fewer large estates and, accordingly, fewer big houses, the figure for burnings was lower, but they still occurred.

The question then arises: what were the motives behind these attacks? Indeed, is it possible to discover whether there was any common ground between one burning and another? Those responsible rarely left behind an explanation for their behaviour, although the leading Cork republican Tom Barry in his own memoir *Guerilla Days in Ireland* explained that 'castles, mansions and residences were sent up in flames by the IRA immediately after the British fire gangs had razed the homes of Irish Republicans'. As far as he was concerned, 'the demesne walls were tumbling and the British ascendancy was being destroyed. Our only fear was that, as time went on, there would be no more Loyalists' homes to destroy, for we intended to go to the bitter end.' Similarly, Ernie O'Malley's *On Another Man's Wound* recalled Liam Lynch, after hearing that a number of houses in North Cork had been blown up by British forces in reprisal for an ambush, had bitterly declared, 'I'll bloody well settle that: six big houses and castles of their friends, the Imperialists, will go up for this.' Reprisal certainly seems to have been a motive on quite a few occasions during both conflicts. In the course of the War of Independence, when the Black and Tans went on one of their periodic rampages, burning swathes of houses in towns and the countryside, the IRA regularly responded by setting fire to the most prominent property in the area. Likewise in the course of the Civil War, when the Free State government began to execute its opponents, the anti-Treaty forces took to burning houses, particularly those owned by senators.

In such cases, attacks on these buildings were just one tactic available to those involved in an armed struggle, but its regular use indicates a long-standing want of engagement with such properties: they were perceived to belong, in Liam Lynch's words, to 'the Imperialists' and had no connection with the rest of the country. House owners might even be judged actively hostile to the native population. When Convamore, County Cork was burnt in May 1921, an explanatory note from the IRA advised this had been ordered because its owner, Lord Listowel, was considered 'an aggressively anti-Irish person'. Two months later, Moydrum Castle, County Westmeath was also left gutted by fire, ostensibly in response to the burning by British forces of several houses owned by IRA sympathizers, but also because Lord Castlemaine, who lived there, was 'a member of the British House of Lords and was always an opponent of Irish National aspirations'.

Sometimes the grievances could be of an older lineage, even going back centuries. In some quarters there existed a residual hatred for house owners, a feeling that they occupied land which had been stolen by their forebears from the native population. A number of owners recognized this. In a letter to the editor of *The Times* published on 22 September 1922 and written after his Irish home, Derreen, County Kerry had been destroyed, the Marquess of Lansdowne declared:

> What is happening, and has happened, is not a conflict in the open between enemies, but the relentless and persistent perse-cution of a helpless minority, which is obnoxious because it is regarded as of alien origin, because it stands for law and order, because its possessions are coveted, and because it is the settled policy of the conspirators to oust it from the country.

Early the following month, the same newspaper carried a letter from the secretary of the Irish Compensation Claims Bureau in London who insisted that 'the process of destruction which has been applied to Lord Lansdowne's residence is only part of a well-organised system which is being applied at the moment all over Ireland for the murder and expulsion of the Irish gentry, their dependents, and all those who have in the past shown any British sympathies'. The *Irish Times*, which quoted from the above letter in an editorial on 3 October 1922, rightly disputed that the burning of Derreen, or indeed any other house, was part of a 'well organised system'. What cannot be called into question, however, is that large sections of the population, particularly in rural areas, regarded country houses and owners as alien presences.

One explanation often advanced for a house being burnt was that it would otherwise be used by the members of the British army or, after their departure, by Free State forces. Country properties were large, usually stoutly built and comfortable and surrounded by open land, providing grounds for drilling as well as making it easy to see the approach of any possible foe. They were, therefore, ripe for seizure, especially once so many RIC stations and military barracks had already been destroyed. Owners found their homes requisitioned by one side or the other, sometimes just for a few days, sometimes longer. When these uninvited guests departed, they might burn out the building to stop it falling into the hands of the opposition; in some instances, even without being occupied, houses were attacked and destroyed on the basis of rumour that they were going to be taken over by the other side. Such seems to have been the case with Tyrone House, County Galway, which had been unoccupied by the St George family for the previous decade. Even if not actually burnt out, houses used in this manner tended to suffer grievous damage: furniture might be smashed, paintings damaged and other items like bed linen and clothing stolen.

Another factor that has to be considered when looking at house burnings was one long potent in Ireland: the hunger for land. By this time, the struggle for its possession had largely, although not completely concluded, the turning point being the 1903 Wyndham Act. This permitted tenants to borrow necessary funds from the British government and use the money to buy out their landlords. In 1870, 97 per cent of the country was owned by landlords: by 1916, 70 per cent of Irish farmers owned their own land. The agricultural revolution happened before its political equivalent. Nevertheless, the majority of country-house owners held onto the demesne immediately surrounding their homes, and these home farms and parklands could run to hundreds, even thousands, of acres. For small farmers still hungry to own, or to enlarge, their own modest parcels of land, one potential means of realizing their ambitions was to burn down a landlord's house, in the understandable expectation that he would then sell up the rest of his estate. In some cases, this did happen. In many other instances, the Free State's Land Commission would soon divide up and parcel out an estate's land, thereby encouraging the owner's departure. On the other hand, agrarian agitation during this period was as often against ranchers and large farmers, the members of both these groups being, like the people opposed to them, overwhelmingly Catholic in faith and nationalist in sympathy. Hunger for land was the issue, and by the early 1920s the old landlords were no longer major players in a struggle that had been going on for at least half a century. Nonetheless, their continuing presence in the countryside was potently symbolic, suggesting the old order had not entirely been overthrown, and that it might yet return. Hence the desire in some quarters to burn down the houses from which the gentry and aristocracy had once held sway over the surrounding countryside: a ruinous shell provided irrefutable evidence that times had changed once and for all.

Plain opportunism cannot be ignored. The breakdown of law and order, the widespread absence of a local police force, the preoccupation of first the British and then the Free State governments with more important matters, meant these buildings were left particularly vulnerable and exposed. Appeals for help from their owners in many cases went unheeded because the relevant authorities had too many other demands on their limited resources. Furthermore, burnings rarely happened all of a sudden. More usually they were the culmination of a long and gradual campaign of encroachment and intimidation. This would perhaps begin with the theft of some agricultural implements or a few trees being cut down, and then, since no retribution appeared forthcoming, gradually escalate until the main house itself was attacked. A series of raids sometimes took place without the property being burned. Those responsible might be looking for guns, or they would seek supplies of food, blankets and so forth. Items taken could on occasion be quite random – clothing or pieces of china – again suggesting a certain degree of opportunism. In a number of instances, valuable silver or paintings were stolen, even furniture, as was the case at Derreen, County Kerry, summer home of the Marquess of Lansdowne. Following the eventual burning of the house there, the behaviour of those responsible was denounced from the pulpit by the local parish priests, with the result that over the coming weeks and months, a variety of goods taken from Derreen were anonymously returned, most often under the cover of darkness. Similarly, while anti-Treaty forces occupied Mitchelstown Castle, County Cork in June 1922, a number of paintings and pieces of silver appear to have left the property. Anticipating an attack from the Free State army, according to Edith Somerville, the castle's illicit residents used books from the library as barricades in the windows '& as there are not enough, valuable old furniture is being used as well'. In the middle of August, they left, but not before setting the castle alight.

Mitchelstown Castle's prominent location, with extensive views of the surrounding countryside, helps to account for its seizure and destruction, but not all burnings can be so easily explained. Spiddal House, County Galway was home to the Morrises, descendants of one of the ancient Tribes of Galway and a family which had remained resolutely loyal to the Roman Catholic faith throughout the Penal Law period. On the other hand, they were also determinedly pro-

Union so this may be why the place was torched in April 1923. The Esmondes, settled for centuries at Ballynastragh, County Wexford were also Roman Catholics, and in addition keen supporters of Home Rule. However, Sir Thomas Esmonde agreed to be a senator in the first Free State Oireachtas, and so his house was burnt by anti-Treaty supporters in March 1923, a particularly grievous loss since it held many treasures, not least the papers of Henry Grattan, as well as correspondence from Charles J. Fox, Daniel O'Connell, William Smith O'Brien, John Mitchell, Charles Stewart Parnell and others: all were lost in the fire. The mediaeval forebears of the Crosbies of Ardfert, County Kerry had been hereditary bards in what is now County Laois and the Keanes of Cappoquin, County Waterford were descended from the O'Cahans, ancient allies of the O'Neills in Ulster. In neither case did these distinguished antecedents protect their property from attack. Of course, some owners were, without question, venal and deservedly unpopular landlords, not least Colonel Charles Warden of Derryquin, County Kerry who over the course of a couple of decades of ownership managed to make himself thoroughly hated in the area. However, there were other house owners against whom it would be difficult to level any criticism, such as the Earl of Desart who, along with other members of his family, had done much to improve conditions in County Kilkenny: his sister-in-law, the dowager Countess of Desart built the model village of Talbot's Inch, as well as a hospital for the local people, paid for a theatre in Kilkenny city as well as providing funds for its Carnegie Library. None of this stopped the burning of Desart Court in February 1923.

Lord Desart's response to this tragedy – a fortnight after the fire, he told his granddaughter, 'The wound is deep and there is no cure for it' – was typical of that articulated by owners. An awareness that this was the work of arsonists, frequently anonymous, made the sense of grief worse: in the aftermath of the attack Lord Desart, like many others who had suffered in the same way, received letters of condolence not dissimilar to those sent to someone who has lost a close family member. The pain was real and profound. Yet hitherto relatively little investigation has been undertaken into the experience of house owners whose properties were burnt during this period. While the bare facts are often well known, how many buildings were attacked, where and when incidents occurred, their individual histories and those of the families who once occupied them, have received much less attention; what were for the owners highly personal tragedies, in which they lost possessions often going back centuries, and with these part of their own identities, have frequently been treated as just one of the incidental misfortunes of warfare.

Until now, fiction has provided almost the only insight into what happened from the perspective of an Irish country house owner. Many of the novels that deal with this subject, the likes of Elizabeth Bowen's *The Last September*, Molly Keane's *Two Days in Aragon* and J.G. Farrell's *Troubles*, conclude with a fire, making this event the culmination of a narrative and accordingly representing it as a foregone conclusion, which was not necessarily the case. While a handful of other works, not least Barbara Fitzgerald's *We Are Besieged* and *The Major's Candlesticks* by George Bermingham, open with a house going up in flames, owing to the demands of fiction, in none of these books is the wider context sufficiently investigated, not least the options then available to families who had suffered damage and loss.

An invaluable source of information on this subject are the claims submitted by property owners seeking financial compensation for what had happened to them. It was an issue that drew on the resources of both the British and Free State governments, not least because while almost every householder would have taken out insurance cover, this specifically excluded damage caused by civil commotion or riot. Hence companies had no obligation to provide financial assistance. The only alternative for owners was to seek compensation under the terms of the 1898 Local Government (Ireland) Act, and supplementary acts of 1918 and 1919. The legislation permitted owners to enter a claim against the council of the county in which the attack had taken place, the case to be heard by a judge in the local court. The funds to cover any compensation paid would, in turn, have to be raised from among the county's ratepayers, and the growing number of such claims from 1919 onwards meant that a further act passed the following year allowed councils to appeal to the Lord Lieutenant should the amount that had to be found for compensation impose 'an excessive burden on the ratepayers'. The Lord Lieutenant could then direct that the sum required be paid out in instalments over not more than five years.

When claims came before county courts, the figure sought was hardly ever granted, and this rankled among many house owners, especially those who felt their claims had not been excessive. After Castle Bernard, County Cork was burnt in June 1921 (and its owner, the Earl of Bandon, kidnapped and held by the IRA for three weeks), a claim of £100,000 for the building and £70,000 for its contents was submitted, but only £62,000 for the former and £14,000 for the latter awarded by the judge. Other house owners received an even less favourable response to their claims. Next came the problem of trying to secure the funds. Initially local councils, almost invariably nationalist dominated, refused to contest court awards. Then they declined to pay the amount allowed, as this would mean handing over hard-pressed ratepayers' money in order that a large country house might be rebuilt. When this occurred, the British government retaliated by deducting the amount due to be paid to property owners from its grant to the relevant local authority.

In the aftermath of the Anglo-Irish Treaty, a new arrangement was proposed whereby each side was to pay compensation for any losses it had inflicted in the pre-truce period and in May 1922 an official body, the Compensation (Ireland) Commission was established. It took over responsibility from local authorities for assessing claims for damage to property during the period January 1919 to July 1921 (when the truce had been declared). The commission, which sat until March 1926, did not provide compensation for losses due to looting or theft, or due to the commandeering of property by either side and damage sustained in consequence: this resulted in much grievance among owners whose houses might not have been burnt but had suffered during the period. Furthermore, once both governments came to understand how substantial the sums involved would be, the commission was inclined to reduce amounts already agreed in a local court, causing further anguish to claimants. By the time the commission finished, it had investigated 40,700 claims worth £19.1 million, but only granted awards in 17,800 cases at a final cost of £7.04 million.

These claims were only for the period up to July 1921, and did not cover damage suffered by property owners during the subsequent Civil War. To handle these, the Free State government passed the Damage to Property (Compensation) Act 1923, which proved just as unpopular among claimants as had the Compensation (Ireland) Commission. Reverting back to an earlier format, money to meet claims once more had to come from the relevant local authority, challenging the likelihood of a sympathetic hearing in court. No claims could be made for loss of personal items such as clothing and jewellery, nor for loss of use of the house or consequential damage while it was left in a ruinous state. No financial assistance was provided if, in the aftermath of fire, an alternative residence had to be bought or rented. Owners seeking compensation for looted goods were required to prove that the people who had taken them were 'engaged in or purporting to act or who might reasonably be presumed to have been acting in the name or on behalf of any combination or conspiracy for the overthrow' of the Provisional government or who belonged to any 'unlawful or seditious association'. Providing such proof was a challenge.

Most problematic for many owners was a clause in the act stating that compensation for damage or destruction would only be forthcoming if the building were wholly reinstated on the same site or partially so in the vicinity. Understandably, a lot of claimants had no wish to continue living in a place where their homes had been burnt, and where they had experienced overt hostility from their neighbours. Some owners, such as Sir John Keane of Cappoquin,

County Waterford did go ahead and rebuild their houses, usually having to find money from additional sources to complete the job. Others, like the Talbot-Crosbies of Ardfert, County Kerry found a way around the issue by reaching an agreement with the government to build homes elsewhere. Almost invariably awards made by county courts were subsequently challenged by the State, which would send its own inspectors to investigate and report on the case. Officialdom, cool and objective, assessed the damage and loss in a manner that did not take personal value into account. An application might, for example, propose that the house in question needed to be rebuilt entirely, whereas an inspector would argue that some of the walls, if these were still standing, could be retained, thereby saving money. Likewise, a number of Office of Public Works employees would examine claims for destroyed furniture, paintings and other such goods, questioning the value that had been placed on these. Houses and their contents were simply objects with a market price: feelings had no place in the matter.

Without fail, the final grant, already lower than had initially been sought, would then be reduced further. The Free State government, with many pressing calls on its meagre resources, was unsurprisingly disinclined to be generous towards country-house owners: however badly the latter had suffered, their circumstances still looked to be better than that of most of the population. In May 1923 the secretary of the Department of Finance, J.J. McElligott, declared that the aim should be 'to be in a position to oppose every claim when it comes up for hearing'.

In these circumstances, quite a few owners could not afford to rebuild, and therefore received very little compensation for the loss of their property. As for those who did go ahead with the reconstruction of their homes, they would find payment painfully slow, leading several claimants to appeal to W.T. Cosgrave, President of the Irish Free State's Executive Council, in the hope that he would intervene in their case: while expressing sympathy, Cosgrave declined to become involved.

Two or more years might pass since a house was burnt before the final settlement was agreed, after which compensation would only be paid out in instalments, and only on receipt of documentation indicating that another stage of rebuilding had taken place. Monies were withheld until claimants' own tax affairs, including the full payment of rates, were deemed to be in order. Even after all this had been done, a regular complaint made by owners, their agents or architects was that while they had provided the necessary paperwork months earlier, the funds were still not forthcoming and workmen were being left unpaid. It sometimes took years before the final payment was made to an owner. Meanwhile, because of the terms of the act, alternative accommodation would have to be found and funded privately, once again without any financial assistance.

Inevitably, some unscrupulous individuals sought to take advantage of the compensation system. At Barbavilla, County Westmeath, Captain Cecil St George Lyster-Smythe managed to secure funds that ought by rights have gone to his mother, while a few miles away a bankrupt entrepreneur, Patrick J. Weymes, tried to improve his financial circumstances by grossly exaggerating the amount of damage inflicted on Clonyn Castle. It does not appear there were too many such attempts to mislead the authorities and, at least in the case of Weymes, the claim's fraudulence was quickly exposed.

Whether applying to the Compensation (Ireland) Commission or to the Free State government through the Damage to Property (Compensation) Act, claimants were required to make an official request using standardized forms. Most of these are now kept in either the British or Irish National Archives and give an invaluable insight into the experience of house owners who suffered the attack and destruction of their property. Claimants needed to provide details of what had happened, and when, a chronological account of incidents with information on the value of anything lost or damaged on each occasion. Some of them were more meticulous than others in chronicling their experiences: Colonel Warden of Derryquin produced a 94-page leather-bound volume that opened with an account of the successive outrages he had experienced before itemizing every last item lost. The inventory for what was destroyed in the fire at Kilboy, County Tipperary in August 1922 runs to forty-two typed pages just for the main house. There are further inventories for other buildings on the estate, together with information on what items of clothing belonging to whom were burnt (a peer's uniform worn by Lord Dunalley was valued at £40, and his peer's coronet was worth a further £10).

Other accounts are more sketchy suggesting owners were unaccustomed to dealing with official documents, or perhaps felt the rightfulness of their claim was so self-evident that it did not require very much elaboration. A great many claimants, obviously finding the official forms too impersonal, included statements testifying to the trauma they had suffered, and its long-term consequences. For quite a few of them, one of those consequences was exile in England, a banishment from what, until then, they had thought – even if others did not – to be their native country. Some were obliged to rely on charitable support from family and friends, and even those lucky enough to have a private income found their means greatly reduced. After Desart Court, County Kilkenny was burnt, its owner the fifth Earl of Desart bought a small property in Sussex and his daughter later wrote of his struggle to become interested in the place. One evening, as the family discussed the creation of a new rock garden, she noticed 'the look of great weariness and deep indifference that came over his face. I knew he was thinking of Desart, of the long borders in the kitchen-garden and the great flowery terrace in the sunset. He could not easily become attached to a garden-plot in Sussex.' Driven out of Bingham Castle, County Mayo, Denis Bingham and his wife bought a house in Dorset which they named Newbrook, after his family's original family home in Ireland. Similarly, after Spiddal House, County Galway was burnt, its owner the second Lord Killanin acquired a house in Hampshire, which he named Galvia, the Latin word for Galway.

These details provide an insight into the feelings of owners whose cherished homes had been lost, as does other material, such as the diary kept by Sir John Keane, a documentary account written by the Earl of Bessborough and a memoir composed by one of Lord Dunalley's sons. Where possible, and where available, this material has been used here to make more vivid the experiences of individuals and families whose properties were destroyed during this period. And the background histories of both places and people have also been included, because whether we like it or not, when flames consumed a building, they also consumed part of Ireland's history. The house contents lost in the same conflagrations, the pictures, the furniture, the silver and so forth: the destruction of these items likewise left the country poorer, and not just materially.

What happened in the aftermath of these fires? A number of owners – like Sir John Keane at Cappoquin, Lord Lansdowne at Derreen and indeed the Bagwells at Marlfield – rebuilt their homes, frequently because they had nowhere else to go, or could not imagine living anywhere but the place where they had been born and raised, like generations of ancestors before them. Some houses, such as Desart Court or Kilboy, were rebuilt but subsequently demolished, the lands on which they had stood purchased by new owners. Others, not least Bessborough, having been scrupulously reconstructed, were similarly sold, their original proprietors believing there was no place for them in post-independence Ireland. The shell of a once-great house like Derryquin or Ardfert Abbey could remain for some time in the aftermath of fire before the site was cleared, so that today it is hard to know a building once stood there. Little now survives of Bingham Castle, which was not burnt but instead seems to have been picked apart over many years, just a handful of low stone walls left to indicate its location.

Even readers who might consider the destruction of so many country houses to be a matter of little importance to Ireland and the greater part of her people, can surely recognize the horror of seeing a house being suddenly and deliberately destroyed. The loss of a family home, regardless of size or age, is a traumatic event. In the instances described here, these were buildings where the owners had spent the greater part of their lives and which, almost without exception, had been occupied for hundreds of years by their ancestors. When the house went up in flames, so did an integral part of their own being. Everything identified with them, all the belongings that had defined who they were, helped to give them their sense of being, had in one brutal moment been taken away. And in the aftermath, they would find themselves left with nothing. Not even a handkerchief.

1

'My Country Broke Me'
SPIDDAL HOUSE, COUNTY GALWAY

IN AUGUST 1927, barely a fortnight after his thirteenth birthday, Michael Morris inherited a comfortable seat in the House of Lords, and a ruined seat in County Galway. Although aware of being in line for both, he had not expected to do so quite so soon. But his unmarried uncle Martin, for whom Spiddal House had been a surrogate child, never recovered from its destruction by fire in 1923 and four years later, just weeks before his own sixtieth birthday, he died alone and unhappy.

The premature assumption of adulthood appears not to have adversely affected Michael Morris, who after five years at Eton College went on to attend Cambridge University. There he managed to find time both to box and to serve as president of the university's dramatic club, the 'Footlights', before becoming in succession a journalist, a member of the British army during the Second World War, a film producer and finally in 1972, the role for which he is best-remembered, president of the International Olympic Committee.

The Morrises were used to holding positions of authority. Since the Middle Ages they had been one of the fourteen Tribes of Galway, a name disparagingly bestowed on the city's leading mercantile families by Cromwellian troops in the mid-seventeenth century. The epithet became a badge of honour, happily embraced by subsequent generations of the Morris clan as a means of marking their long association with Galway, begun in 1485 when a forebear, Richard Morris, was appointed bailiff of the city. Several of his descendants occupied the same position, as well as that of mayor, until the surrender of Galway to members of the scornful Cromwellian army in 1652: Andrew Morris was one of the few Tribesmen who refused to sign an order of capitulation to the enemy. Later his grandson George Morris would serve under James II against the forces of William III.

Thereafter little is heard of the Morrises for at least a century. In 1684 George had married Catherine Fitzpatrick, an heiress whose father John owned the Aran Islands; as part of her marriage settlement, she brought with her land around Spiddal, a coastal village some eighteen kilometres west of Galway city. The Morris family now settled there, steadfastly remaining Roman Catholic and, as a result of the Penal Laws, prohibited from holding public office. So they stayed quiet, intermarrying with members of other descendants of the Tribes of Galway, the Blakes and Brownes and Lynches, who like them had moved to the country, acquired land and bided their time.

It came with the gradual dismantling of the Penal Laws, the last of them repealed in 1829. All public positions were once more open to Catholics and among the first to take advantage of this liberalization was Martin Morris of Spiddal. Born in 1784, he became a Justice of the Peace for the county, and in 1841 was appointed High Sheriff of Galway, the first Catholic to hold the position since 1690. Almost twenty years before assuming the office, he had married Julia Blake, whose family, like his own, were part of the original Tribes of Galway. Before her sudden death from cholera after just eleven years of marriage, Julia had four children, the eldest of whom would restore the Morrises to their former prominence.

Born in November 1826, Michael Morris was still only sixteen when he entered Trinity College Dublin: his religion disqualified him from competing for the scholarship he would otherwise certainly have won. At twenty he graduated as first senior moderator in Ethics and

Logic, and won a gold medal. Having travelled abroad for a year, he studied law and was called to the Irish Bar in 1849. Professional success quickly followed. As the *Dictionary of National Biography* later noted, 'His rise in his profession was rapid, his abounding commonsense, his wit, and strong Galway brogue, which never diminished, attracted clients.' Not everyone was necessarily charmed by Michael Morris's brogue, his wife's cousin Edgar L'Estrange later writing: 'He had an exaggerated Galway accent, which he cultivated to such an extent, that he appeared ridiculous. He indulged in low meaningless witticisms ...' (On the other hand, L'Estrange appears to have disliked most people, including his own children. When compiling a family memoir in 1901, he wrote of his three sons – all of whom had emigrated to Australia – that they 'have been for so many years associated with and acquired the habits and ideas of descendants of criminals of the worst type ... they will probably not appreciate my trouble'.)

Like his father before him, in 1849 Michael Morris served as High Sheriff of Galway. In 1865 he was elected MP for Galway in the Westminster Parliament, receiving some 90 per cent of the vote even though he belonged to no party. The next year he was appointed Solicitor-General for Ireland, the first Catholic to hold the post in a Conservative government, and later the same year he became Attorney-General for Ireland and a member of the Irish Privy Council. In 1887 he was made Lord Chief Justice of Ireland. Already created a baronet in 1885, four years later he was promoted to the judicial committee of the English Privy Council, receiving a life peerage with the title Lord Morris. When he retired from this last position in 1900, he accepted an hereditary peerage and was thereafter known as Lord Killanin.

It was, without doubt, a dazzling career, and one ably supported by Michael Morris's wife. Anna Hughes was the elder daughter of Henry George Hughes, whose own professional history was not unlike that of his future son-in-law. A Roman Catholic, he also attended Trinity College Dublin before becoming a lawyer, soon building up a large and successful practice. Appointed Solicitor-General for Ireland in 1850, six years later he was elected a Member of Parliament for Longford where he had acquired an estate. At the time of his death in 1872, the *Irish Law Times* described him as 'courteous, painstaking, upright and eminently sagacious'.

His daughter Anna was nineteen when she married Michael Morris, fourteen years her senior, in 1860. Around this time, or soon after, the couple acquired the house in Spiddal where they and their children would spend several months every summer. The family already owned land in the area, but following the death of his wife in 1833, Michael Morris's father had moved to Galway city and never returned to a place he associated with a happy but too-short marriage. So it was only after his own marriage that the young lawyer brought his bride to Spiddal where he had spent his earliest years. The house they bought dated from the first years of the nineteenth century and was originally called Bohoona Lodge. Relatively small, it was essentially a holiday home without pretentions to grandeur. Over the next couple of decades, the building grew steadily larger because Michael and Anna Morris had thirteen children, ten of whom survived to adulthood. One of them, Maud, later remembered 'my mother loved dabbling in stones and mortar, and the interest would hasten her convalescence, for after each baby she would add on an extra room here and there, until the house became a sort of rabbit warren'.

Spiddal House, as it became known, was the place Michael Morris loved best and, as Maud wrote, 'Every moment that my father could spare from his judicial work in Dublin, and later on in London, was spent at Spiddal, as he said he only went to England to make money and came home to spend it.' Twice daily he would walk to the pier for the construction of which he had provided funds in 1868 (in the misplaced hope that Spiddal would become a major fishing port) and, filling his lungs, exclaim: 'Who wants to go to Biarritz with this air, it is much better than Biarritz.'

The appeal of the area is easy to understand, and fortunately was shared by his wife; her two passions were swimming and fishing. Not everyone shared their enthusiasm. Although Spiddal is little more than ten miles from Galway city, in the nineteenth century it appears to have been barely touched by modernity. There was no train service until 1895, journeys before that date having to be taken along the only road in the district in an old-fashioned coach. Most of the local people were exceedingly poor and few of them spoke English. During the summer of 1888 Violet Martin, one half of the Somerville and Ross writing partnership, came to lunch at Spiddal House. Nothing, she told Edith Somerville, 'could explain the length of those 11 Irish miles, or the loneliness of the road. It was like mid ocean and a slight mist tended to increase the unboundedness of the stretches of moor and bog.' As a result, when she reached the Morris house, it had 'the feeling of Russian magnificence in Siberia'.

So it must have seemed to the majority of people living in the vicinity, with the Morrises appearing to revel in princely affluence. Around this time, following Michael Morris's appointment as a new Lord of Appeal, they were required to spend time in London. There they took a house in Grosvenor Crescent (ranked in 2017 as Britain's most expensive residential street), living a short distance from Buckingham Palace and mixing with members of the Royal Family: Michael Morris was much liked by the Prince of Wales (the future Edward VII). But they still spent several months annually in Spiddal where improvements were made to bring the house up to the standards of London. A new bathroom was built and a large bath ordered. The very first to be installed in Connemara, the bath was brought from Galway in a cart pulled by two horses, its stately progress through the countryside followed by locals with wonder and excitement. When finally in place, Anna Morris invited one of her favourite outdoor labourers, Mark Curran, to see the bath. He stood silently before it for some time before asking: 'And will ye all get in together?'

Spiddal House might have been more luxurious than anywhere else in the vicinity, but it was not necessarily happier. After Michael Morris died in 1901, the Marquess of Dufferin and Ava described him as 'a representative in his handsome person, in his wit, in the grace of his manners and his indomitable gaiety of those engaging characteristics which generally distinguish an ancient Celtic line'. Charming and witty in public, Michael Morris was frequently moody and difficult in private. Writing in 1937, his daughter Maud remembered that while Spiddal ought to have been a paradise for children, 'our childhood had nothing heavenly about it … The atmosphere was too tense and dramatic, and children, like animals, thrive best in a peaceful, matter-of-fact, monotonous world.' She and her siblings were never sure when the next explosion from their father would come, leaving them forever anxious and uneasy. Every second Tuesday he would have to leave Spiddal and be driven to Galway, from there to take a train to Dublin to chair a meeting of the Board of National Education. 'How we enjoyed those fortnightly Tuesdays,' recalled Maud, 'as the tense atmosphere melted away. Everyone from my mother down to the garden boy relaxed visibly.'

Inevitably, there were consequences. A few years after leaving school, the couple's eldest daughter Lily became a nun and cut herself off from the world in which she had been raised. Dying at the age of twenty-eight, 'she cared to see none of her own family, even in her last illness – all her interests were elsewhere or with her religious sisters'. Two of the other Morris daughters likewise became nuns, joining the enclosed Carmelite order as though, like Lily, they wished to escape their own family. Of the Morris sons, two died young, one of them Redmond at twenty-five, just as he had embarked on a legal career that promised to match that of his father. Saddest of all was the youngest child, Charles Ambrose, who at eighteen had won a scholarship to Balliol College Oxford. However, soon after taking his place he disappeared, catching a train to France where he shot himself leaving a letter for his mother in which he told her 'it is no good. Nothing can give me the courage to bear any more life. I have gone away and the best I can hope for is that you will never know where.' His body was discovered in Dijon and there he was buried.

Another son would also die in France. George Henry Morris had passed straight from school into the Royal Military College, Sandhurst. His military career began with several years in India before he saw active service during the second Boer War. Returning to England, he was transferred to the newly formed Irish Guards and became the commander of its 1st Battalion in 1913. At the onset of the First World War in mid-August 1914 Lieutenant-Colonel Morris led his troops to France: just over two weeks later, on 1 September, he was killed during the retreat from Mons. He left behind a widow and a son born only a month earlier: that boy, called Michael Morris after his grandfather, would become the third Lord Killanin in 1927.

This occurred following the death of his uncle Martin, who had succeeded to the title, and the Spiddal estate in 1901. Like many of his siblings, Martin Morris seems to have been an unhappy and unfulfilled individual: his sister Maud thought he had led 'a tragic lonely life of shattered ideals'. His early years promised otherwise. The eldest son of brilliant, much-admired parents, after school in England he went to Trinity College Dublin where he became secretary of the University Philosophical Society (the world's oldest such student club). In 1890 the university's press published one of the papers he had read to members of the Society the previous year, and for which he had been awarded the President's Gold Medal. *Religion and Science: or The Spiritual and the Material in Life* is essentially a debate on the respective merits of religion and science, the former ultimately being judged worthy of first place. Along the way, the author displays his wide reading, a distinct fondness for the likes of Ralph Waldo Emerson and Thomas Carlyle being seasoned by an awareness of the then-fashionable aesthetic precepts of Walter Pater. His essential caution manifests itself when he insists, 'Let us not be intoxicated by the material wonders of this age, nor believe that anything, dealing with the great and important mysteries of Life, has been in any way solved or even improved. Science will never solve man's destiny.'

The same set of beliefs was outlined in *Life's Greatest Possibility: an Essay in Spiritual Realism* published anonymously two years later. This short book was widely if not altogether favourably reviewed, the *Irish Times* critic observing that while the text was 'the outcome of somewhat perplexed metaphysical reflections' nevertheless it breathed 'wholesome thought' and so would be read 'with pleasure by an educated class, which, as a rule, learns philosophy at second hand from the persiflage popular literature of the time'.

Martin Morris, it appears, had notions of becoming an author, along the lines of his idol Emerson. In fact, he published only one further volume, *Transatlantic Traits*, which came out in 1897. A garbled account of a recent trip made with a friend to the United States, the book attempts to draw from this visit the distinctive characteristics of the American people, none of which seem to have impressed him much. It was not well received and effectively ended Martin Morris's literary career. Evidently he recognized this to be the case, since he had by now followed his father's example and been called to the Bar. Again like his father before him, in 1900 he was elected as an Member of Parliament for Galway but had to resign his seat a year later when, following Michael Morris's death, he became the second Lord Killanin and took his seat in the House of Lords.

Although he published nothing more, Martin Morris maintained links with the Irish literary movement. Lady Gregory, an old family friend, had for many years come to Spiddal for a spell every summer, and it was one of the places where she learned to understand and speak the Irish language. Through her, the family met W.B. Yeats. In the summer of 1896 Martin Morris gave his verdict of the poet to Violet Martin who in turn reported to her cousin Edith Somerville that Yeats was 'a little affected – and knows it – He has a sense of humour and is a gentleman – hardly by birth I think – but by genius.'

Yeats had come to Connemara after staying at Tulira Castle, County Galway. This belonged to one of his co-founders (together with Lady Gregory) of the Irish National Theatre, Edward Martyn. A devout Catholic, Martyn was responsible for commissioning much of the decoration of St Brendan's Cathedral in Loughrea, barely ten miles from his family home. The cathedral is perhaps the single greatest repository of Celtic Revival work in Ireland, its stained glass provided by the An Túr Gloine studio, banners and vestments made by the Dun Emer Guild, and carvings by sculptors such as Michael Shortall and John Hughes. Also involved in the project was the foremost architect working in Ireland at the start of the last century, William Alphonsus Scott. Having trained first with his father and then with Sir Thomas Newenham Deane, followed by a period in London, Scott set up his own practice in Dublin and soon began receiving significant commissions and equally significant acclaim, being described by W.B. Yeats – for whom he restored and furnished the medieval tower house at Thoor Ballylee – as 'the drunken man of genius' although there is no evidence that his alcohol intake was particularly prodigious.

His output, on the other hand, certainly was considerable, and included a new Catholic church at Spiddal, commissioned by Martin Morris who laid the building's foundation stone in 1904. Today considered Scott's masterpiece, St Enda's is both an evocation and reinterpretation of Hiberno-Romanesque ecclesiastical design and was immediately acclaimed, Edward Martyn declaring it 'the first incoming wave of what we may hope to be a fresh vigorous tide of architecture in Ireland'.

The Spiddal church led to a wave of further commissions, not least from his patron there, Martin Morris. As noted by the latter's sister Maud, the family house had expanded higgledy-piggledy around the modest lodge acquired by their parents in the early 1860s. As Lord Killanin, and as a patron of the arts, Martin Morris decided to bring coherence to his residence, and in 1908 invited Scott to reorder both the main building and its surroundings. Work first began on a new triple-arched entrance and adjacent castellated lodge; these gave access to a drive through the grounds and over a stone bridge designed by Scott with seats set into miniature turrets that offered views of the River

Owenboliska below. In July 1909 the *Irish Builder* announced work was about to start on 'alterations and extensions to Spiddal House for Lord Killanin, in accordance with designs prepared by Mr W.A. Scott'.

Finished two years later at a cost of some £10,000, the result was unlike anything else in Connemara, and caused as much of a stir as had the first bath in the area twenty years before. An unlikely but successful synthesis of the Hiberno-Romanesque and the Byzantine, the house's main entrance was moved to what had hitherto been one side of the building, and was marked by a three-storey tower topped with a domed belvedere. Open loggias to the left of this wrapped around to what became the garden front, with views across terraced lawns to the sea. At the far end ran a colonnade with another arcaded loggia. One of the most distinctive features of the building were the capitals and corbels above arches supporting the loggia columns: these were carved by sculptor Michael Shortall, who had previously worked at Loughrea Cathedral, and they depict Martin Morris and his friends going about various activities, whether playing tennis or making music. Inside, the house was described as containing 'every modern convenience', a later report noting:

> It was not like a house in the wilderness, it was as modern a house as could be found in any county, equipped with hot and cold water and with electric light. It had something like 20 bedrooms, 3 magnificent reception rooms, a large billiard room furnished with billiard table and accessories, and contained 5 bathrooms and a kitchen with three ranges.

At the time of the 1911 census, six staff were resident in the house, including a butler, footman, cook, two housemaids and a fifteen-year-old kitchen maid. Unfortunately, few photographs exist to show how the interior of the building looked following the completion of Scott's work there. But it is clear that the reordering of Spiddal House provided Martin with an opportunity to express his own character, and to put his stamp on a place which had, until then, represented his parents' tastes rather than his own. Now he not only owned the house, but it owed its appearance to him. His abortive literary career, his interest in supporting a new cultural movement: these were made manifest in Spiddal House. For the next ten years, it would be where he was happiest and most at ease.

In the light of the fate that would soon befall the building, it is worth noting that the Morrises, both father and son, were ardently pro-Union and anti-Home Rule. Given the family's history of opposition to Cromwell and support for James II, as well as their abiding loyalty to Catholicism, the position appears unusual, even perverse, but it was genuinely and deeply held. Both men were devoted to their own country and her welfare, Michael Morris famously declaring that England's difficulties with Ireland arose from 'a slow-witted race trying to govern a quick-witted one'. However, both men were also conservative in character, supported the Conservative Party (Michael Morris loathed the Liberal leader William Gladstone as 'the incarnation of much mischief in Ireland') and were members of the Irish Unionist Alliance, speaking in Parliament in favour of maintaining their country's links with Britain. They believed that breaking ties with their wealthier neighbour would leave Ireland weak and in no position to survive economically. For Martin Morris, Home Rule was anathema, and he stated so in speeches made in the House of Lords.

Nevertheless, he continued to be popular locally, for twenty-one years elected a member of the County Council, as well as serving as Lord Lieutenant for Galway. Like his father before him, he was a member of the Board of Education, and in August 1920 was appointed chairman of a government commission to investigate possible improvements in the condition and positions of primary school teachers in Ireland. Issued the following year, the Killanin report led to significant improvements in teachers' pay.

The first sign of trouble came in December 1919, by which date the War of Independence was well under way. Known to share his employer's unionist sympathies, the chauffeur employed at Spiddal, James Ruttledge, lived with his family in a house on the grounds of the estate. One night after Christmas he was visited by five local IRA men, who removed two guns and boxes of ammunition from the premises. When he tried to stop them, he was attacked and beaten about the head with a stick. Many years later the leader of the group insisted: 'The raid was not at all directed against Killanin.' Nor is this likely to have been the case in September 1922 when, during the Civil War, a number of armed men raided Spiddal House, and carried off goods subsequently valued as being worth £151 and thirteen shillings. Most likely the raiders were members of the anti-Treaty forces who, lacking even the limited resources of the new Irish state, regularly descended on private homes to seize whatever they could, be it arms, clothing, food or goods that could later be traded for cash. Maud Morris, by now married to Captain Graham Wynne and living in County Sligo, was woken by late-night raiders on several occasions; eventually the couple decided to leave Ireland for good. '"It's not good enough," said my husband, and it wasn't.'

The raid on Spiddal House greatly upset Martin Morris, already dismayed by the rupture of Ireland's union with Britain, having consistently argued in favour of its retention. The violence displayed during both the War of Independence and the Civil War appalled him, as did the hatred of Britain now made manifest: this was not the Ireland he and his siblings thought they knew. Although still devoted to Spiddal, he began to spend less time there, preferring to be in London. But he evidently felt his home to be safe from attack, since the Morris family had always been well-liked in the area and generous benefactors of churches, schools and convents. There was no hostility towards Martin, despite his support for the Union.

Nevertheless, in early spring 1923, James Dillon, who was employed as general factotum at Spiddal House, received a series of threatening, anonymous letters, accusing him of being a spy and telling him to clear out of the area. One undated document told Dillon he had until 1 March to be gone, otherwise 'you will suffer believe that or not we will dagged (sic) to bits or we will riddle you with bullets + will set the building two (sic) fire + burn it to ashes ...' Dillon remained in situ, a later, similarly anonymous letter giving him until 1 May to leave Spiddal. This one, while advising 'don't think we have anything against Lord K's atall' suggested that during the War of Independence, 'you did your very best the time of black and tans + we remember that time for you yet don't think we have it forgotten atall ...' Hints in these documents suggest the source of trouble was Dillon looking after his employer's interests, especially with regard to fishing rights in the area. He remained at Spiddal, and continued to mind the property. However, on 21 April 1923 Martin wrote to Raoul Joyce, his agent in Galway, asking the latter to call over to Spiddal and check that all was well with Dillon, who had been attacked and beaten a few days earlier.

Disaster struck within the week. By April 1923 the spate of country-house burnings initiated the previous year by anti-Treaty forces had come to an end, not least because their numbers were greatly depleted and exhausted: their Chief of Staff Frank Aitken would eventually call a ceasefire on 30 April. Just two days before, Spiddal House was gutted by fire.

On 11 April, following instructions from the government, six anti-Treaty supporters were executed in Tuam, County Galway. (Since the previous November, the Free State government had operated a policy of executing opponents in order to hasten the war's conclusion: some seventy-seven men so died.) It appears to have been in retaliation for the Tuam executions that republican activists decided to burn down a well-known property. Led by a number of men from Mayo, they travelled to Spiddal, arriving at the house in the early hours of the morning and smashing the glass in the upper portion of the back hall door. The noise awoke the housekeeper, Alice Hopper, who, on coming downstairs, was confronted by a group of men armed with guns who, through the now broken glass panels, ordered her to remove an iron bar impeding their access to the building. Fearing she would be shot,

Alice did as told, and immediately the men rushed past her, all of them carrying petrol tins and buckets from the yard filled with paraffin oil. They said she had ten minutes to collect what she wanted before the house was set alight. By now the cook, Mrs Lee, had also appeared from her room, and while the men began sprinkling fuel around the house, the two servants seized whatever was closest to hand and easiest to carry. In her account of Spiddal House's destruction, Maud Wynne proposes that the women rescued items of greatest interest to them

> so the cook's heart was with her treasures in the kitchen, and Alice's heart was in her linen cupboard. The cook ran downstairs to the kitchen and collecting pots and pans and rolling pins, not forgetting a hair sieve, soon had them out of the window. Alice made straight for her linen cupboard, and here the five or ten golden minutes were spent throwing linen out of the window on to the lawn below, including cretonne covers for the sofa and chairs about to be burnt, blankets and pillows for the beds about to be burnt, and numerous curtains for the windows soon to be in ruins.

The account is amusing, but unfair. 'I got into the drawingroom,' Alice later testified, 'and cleared out all the furniture I could. The fire was springing in through the doors; all the doors and windows were open [in order to create a draught and make the flames spread faster], we saved chairs and stuff out of the drawingroom, and some diningroom chairs and a table.' Afterwards she compiled a list of what had been rescued and while this contains two copper pans and a fish kettle, there is no mention of rolling pins and sieves, nor of quantities of redundant bed linen or curtains.

Fire soon took hold of the building, assisted by the fact that the principal reception rooms and staircase hall were panelled in wood, which quickly caught light. The following day Alice Hopper wrote an account to her employer, telling how she had suddenly remembered that most of the good silver was in a box in her bedroom:

It went very hard to be lost. I had gone downstairs and thought of it at the side door. I rushed back, one of the men met me in the passage going back, he told me if anything happened me he would not be responsible for it. At that time the house was burning furiously over my bedroom and the place covered with smoke. We got so little time to get dressed that it was impossible to save anything only what was at your hand.

Two days later she wrote again. By this time, the heat had died down and inside the building 'the wreckage is fully five feet from the ground'. Behind a heavy iron door, Spiddal House's strongroom and its safe had survived, although all the bottles of wine inside were destroyed, the heat having caused most of them to explode. The top of the strongroom was taken off and a man lowered in to rescue what he could. 'The good breakfast china are all safe,' Alice reassured Martin, 'also the afternoon china and the coffee service. There are a good many tumblers, decanters, also three glass jugs.'

At the time of the fire Martin was in Dinard, Brittany, recovering from a bad dose of flu. The first he learnt of the catastrophe was an account hastily written by James Dillon a few hours after the attack. 'My Lord, we don't know what to do,' this letter ends. 'We are all here heartbroken, and the children are crying.' News of Spiddal House's fate, widely reported in the press, devastated its owner. Only a couple of weeks before he had written to Raoul Joyce, 'I would rather the house destroyed than my employees hurt in looking after it,' but at the time such an event was theoretical. When it actually happened, the shock was profound, not least because of what had been lost, such as the contents of the library. Many of the five thousand or so books in it had belonged to his father, but these had been supplemented by his own collection of ancient texts. Of particular significance was a handsome bible presented to the Morrises by Cardinal Newman, who had written a long inscription to the family inside its cover. Similarly Martin's sister Maud remembered that kept in the drawing room under glass was the gold collar worn by their father as Chief Justice of Ireland; it too was lost.

As so often, the list of goods destroyed in the fire makes for dispiriting reading, not least because it reflected monetary rather than sentimental value. In the entrance hall an old mahogany grandfather clock with brass fittings was deemed to be worth £10 and a mid-seventeenth-century map of Galway £12, but neither figure took into account that these were heirlooms gone forever. Room after room, the pieces were methodically listed and priced. At the start of June, Alice Hopper put in her own claim for items lost in the fire: three pairs of shoes, three nightdresses, three pairs of stockings, two pairs of steel knitting needles, one umbrella, one prayer book and so forth. The total came to some £24. Martin paid it as he did a smaller claim made by James Dillon.

Meanwhile something had to be done with the furniture and other goods salvaged from the fire. Temporarily stored in a room in Dillon's house, they were soon afterwards offered locally at auction, but many potential bidders were intimidated by threats of violence, and lots which ought to have made a total of over £2000 went for less than £700.

A large envelope survives from this period: written on the cover are the words 'Letters of Sympathy'. Inside are numerous notes and cards sent to Martin in the aftermath of Spiddal House being burnt. The second Lord Ashbourne, whose father, like Martin's own, had been a successful Irish lawyer, wrote: 'I need hardly say how much we feel it when we think of the many happy days we have spent there with you.' Lord Fitzalan, the last Lord Lieutenant of Ireland, declared 'We are so distressed to hear about Spiddal, & I sympathise with you very much … it is more hard you should be hit just now when things look as though they may be going to improve.'

The recurrence of phrases like 'deep regret' and 'greatest sympathy' make the letters read like those written when offering condolences on a bereavement. And indeed for Martin, the destruction of Spiddal House represented a kind of death, not just of his home but of his feelings for

Ireland. A week after the fire, he wrote confidentially to Raoul Joyce, 'let me tell you from the beginning what is my intention, that my aim is to get rid of absolutely everything at Spiddal ...' The destruction of his home killed the love he had felt for his country, and for Connemara. 'He never recovered from the sadness and hopelessness of Ireland's fate,' his sister wrote ten years after her brother had died, 'and when his beloved Spiddal was burnt, he seemed to lose his grip on life.'

This account is borne out by a document produced by his lawyers in 1924 when Martin sought compensation for the burning of Spiddal the year before:

> Lord Killanin suffered in body and mind by this appalling outrage, and he has been since then an ill and broken man, and is now a permanent invalid. Faced with the necessity put before him by his legal advisers, when the claim was brought forward in the County Court, of declaring whether he would re-instate Spiddal, he decided in the negative. 'It could never,' in his own words, 'again be a home to me. It is not as though it had been burnt by accident. All old sentiments, affections and associations are broken and outraged in a way impossible to describe, by raids, the brutal beating of and injuries to my employees, and the destruction generally of my estate. If rebuilt, I could never eat a bit of bread again in it with relish. It horrifies one to think of ever having to see it, much less stay there five minutes – the dearer a place was the stronger are such feelings. Even for letting purposes I could not undertake again the anxious job of building and especially after such trying experiences and with such recollections, and at my age, fifty-eight, and with shattered health. I could say like Dr Murray the writer in Dublin the other day, I am broke and my country broke me.'

Martin never returned to Ireland, and described himself as being 'in exile'. He moved between London and a house on the Hampshire coast. There he died on 22 July 1927, three weeks before his sixtieth birthday.

Soon after the fire, Martin's lawyers submitted a claim to the relevant British authorities, seeking compensation for damage to Spiddal House and its contents. The process moved slowly forward. Martin had sought a sum of £22,497 and three shillings. This included £15,598 for rebuilding the main house, £3000 for furniture (plus a further £1380 for furniture which had been sold too cheap at the local auction) and £2100 for loss of the use of his property for several years. Six months after his death, in January 1928 an award was finally made of £9500, together with £100 towards legal costs. By this time, the beneficiary was Martin's thirteen-year-old nephew Michael, now the third Lord Killanin and a schoolboy at Eton. In the event, unlike his uncle he did decide to go ahead and rebuild the family home at Spiddal. His architect was Ralph Henry Byrne, who like Scott before him was responsible for designing a number of Catholic churches. The reconstructed house was simpler in style than its predecessor, without some of the more striking features such as the domed belvedere on top of the main entrance. It served as a family home for the next generation of Morrises, as Michael pursued his diverse career while he and his wife Mary raised their four children. When John Ford came to Ireland to film *The Quiet Man*, he relied on Michael Morris – the two men had met in the United States before the Second World War – and Spiddal House was often visited by the director, as well as John Wayne and Maureen O'Hara. Eventually Michael sold the property and its remaining land in June 1978; today it remains a private home. But the Morris family retains a connection with Spiddal. Ironically, given their long-standing devotion to Roman Catholicism, today their home in the village is the former Church of Ireland church.

2

'I was one of what was termed the Landlord Class'
BINGHAM CASTLE, COUNTY MAYO

IN HIS INTRODUCTION to a reissue of John Bingham's thriller *My Name is Michael Sibley* in 2000, novelist John le Carré confirmed that the late author (who died in 1988) 'had been one of two men who had gone into the making of George Smiley. Nobody who knew John and the work he was doing could have missed the description of Smiley in my first novel.' In fact, few people who knew Bingham were aware that for decades he had worked for Britain's MI5; his previous job had been as a feature writer and then picture editor for the *Sunday Dispatch* newspaper. Nor was it widely known that he was the seventh Baron Clanmorris of Newbrook; in August 1800 his forebear John Bingham, hitherto representing Tuam, County Mayo in the Irish House of Commons, had supported the Act of Union with Great Britain and in return received £8000 and a peerage.

The Binghams had arrived in Ireland in the mid-sixteenth century. *The Peerage of England, Scotland and Ireland*, published in London in 1790, decisively states that the family 'is of Saxon origin, and of very great antiquity, as appears in their pedigree, by the College of Arms; this family was settled at Sutton-Bingham, in the county of Somerset, from whence it removed, and was settled at Binghams Melcombe, in the county of Dorset, where a branch of the family continues to reside.' Whether of such great antiquity or not, it is certainly true that by the twelfth century there were Binghams in Somerset: one of them, Robert de Bingham, became Bishop of Salisbury in 1229 and was responsible for progressing work on its cathedral, in the nave of which can still be seen his tomb. A nephew, also called Robert, married a Dorset heiress and moved to that county, settling at Melcombe where descendants remained in residence until 1895.

More than 350 years earlier, Richard Bingham was born in Binghams Melcombe, youngest son of yet another Robert Bingham. Having a number of older siblings, he was obliged to make his own way, becoming a soldier and naval commander even before the age of twenty. For much of the 1570s he was in mainland Europe fighting in various campaigns before coming to Ireland in 1579 to assist English forces in the suppression of the second Desmond Rebellion launched by the FitzGeralds in Munster. Five years later, Elizabeth I granted him a knighthood and appointed him Governor of Connacht. By this date two of his brothers, George and John, had joined him in Ireland, the first being made Governor of Sligo, the second acting as captain of Sir Richard's garrison. As for the latter, for the greater part of the rest of his life he was engaged in armed struggle for control of this part of Ireland, responding to all opposition with a savagery that is still recalled in the west of Ireland. He died in his seventieth year in Dublin, and, his body having been brought back to England, was buried in Westminster Abbey where a monument declares that having been made Governor of Connacht, he 'suppressed divers rebellions, and that with little charges to Her Ma'ttie, maintaining that province in flourishing estate by the space of 13 years'.

In a memoir of her family published in 1915 Rose McCalmont (*née* Bingham) wrote sympathetically of her forebear, but others understandably have judged him more harshly. As early as 1621, the exiled soldier and writer Philip O'Sullivan Beare in his *Catholic History of Ireland* could declare:

Richard Bingham, Knight, an Englishman, and the Queen's president of the province of Connaught, began his administration with such mildness and moderation that he was most acceptable to all, and the Connaughtmen gave him the honourable title of the Kind President. However, this was not a real but a feigned benignity; not the simplicity of the dove, but of the fox. After he had established a great reputation for kindness and goodness, the heretic broke out into more than Phalaric cruelty, greedily spilling the blood of the Catholics. He hanged O'Connor Roe, aged about 80 years, and slaughtered many of the O'Connors and Burkes.

Most later assessments have been equally critical.

Sir Richard having no male heir, the lands he acquired in Ireland passed to a nephew, Henry Bingham, son of George, Governor of Sligo. Henry, created a baronet in 1634, was the first of the family to settle in Castlebar, County Mayo, a town which he and his successors did much to develop; in 1795 his descendant Charles Bingham would be created first Earl of Lucan.

Sir Henry's brother John Bingham settled in the same part of the country, acquiring large amounts of land around the town of Foxford, which the family owned; it was John Bingham's descendant who became first Baron Clanmorris in 1800. The family seat at Newbrook, some twenty miles south of Foxford, was described by William Wilson in *The Post-Chaise Companion or Travellers Directory through Ireland* (published 1786) as being the 'elegant and delightful seat of Henry Bingham'. This house accidentally burnt down in 1837 and was not rebuilt although the yard buildings remain. In her *Memoirs of the Binghams* Rose McCalmont wrote that the building had been

before that unfortunate event, a typical Irish County house. In form it was nearly square, and doubtless when inhabited contained spacious rooms, though apparently these were not very lofty. The place caught fire in October 1837 and burnt for no less than eight

days. Water in plenty probably was available, but the absence of
appliances for extinguishing fire precluded all hopes of saving the
place until too late.

Lady McCalmont, a daughter of the fourth Lord Clanmorris, was
born too late to have seen Newbrook for herself, but she knew Bingham
Castle, which belonged to cousins of her family. The house was located
in the north-west corner of Mayo on the Erris Peninsula. For centuries
this part of the country had belonged to the Barrett and Bourke families
but in the early 1660s Charles II granted a large portion of the land
here to the Royal Goldsmith Sir Robert Vyner, from whom the king had
borrowed money. Vyner in turn sold it on to Sir James Shaen, Surveyor
General of Ireland who then bequeathed it to his only son, Arthur.
When Sir Arthur died in 1725 he left two daughters, joint heiresses,
the elder of which, Frances Shaen, married in 1738 John Bingham of
Newbrook. Her younger sister Susanna married Henry Boyle Carter of
Castlemartin, County Kildare. Between them, the Binghams and Carters
thereby acquired some 95,000 acres of land in Erris, albeit much of it
bog and mountain and deemed of little agricultural value.

John Bingham's grandson, Denis Bingham, was responsible for
building Bingham Castle. His father, (John's son) Henry, had died in
December 1789 and in his will he stated:

> I give and devise the fee and inheritance of my said Sheane estate
> to my 3rd son Denis Bingham, Lieutenant of his Majesty's 5th
> Dragoon Guards in Ireland, and his heirs male for ever, with
> power to him to settle £100 a year for every £1000 he gets by any
> lady he chooses to marry, and in case he dies without issue male
> my will is that it reverts to my second son Henry Bingham, Esq.,
> and his right heirs for ever, subject to my debts and my sister's
> annuity arising out of the following lands, lying and being in the
> half barony of Erris, Co. Mayo, of my undivided moiety of the
> town and lands of Tumbeagh, etc ...

He also left Denis all his pictures, prints, books and bookcases, with a request that he should 'take care of them in memory of his father', along with two old rings 'that belonged to my mother's family'. All these items remained in Bingham Castle until the mid-1920s.

As his father's will noted, Denis Bingham had been a major in the 5th Dragoon Guards. In her history of the family, Rose McCalmont records that at some date and as a result of a dispute during a parliamentary election, Denis fought a duel with someone called Lord Browne, 'who was reputed to be a dead shot'. On his way to the meeting place, the major's horse stumbled and he was thrown. His superstitious servant immediately advised, 'Turn back, sir, you will surely be dead,' to which the major responded, 'No! I go to live.' In due course the two combatants faced each other and when the signal was given, 'Major Bingham fired so quickly that Lord Browne was dead before firing.'

This story muddles two incidents. A duel took place in Mayo in 1790, arising from an exchange of insults between two candidates in an election: John Bingham, a relation of the Earl of Lucan, and Denis Browne, son of the second Earl of Altamont. When the combatants met, Bingham having missed him with his two bullets, Browne fired into the air, declaring that had he done otherwise, 'he must have mortally wounded his Antagonist'. (Browne also went on to win the election.) On the other hand, in September 1801, during the first election after the Act of Union had been passed, Denis Bingham fought a duel against James Moore O'Donel of Newport, County Mayo. According to a report carried that month by the *Sporting Magazine*, 'Both parties fired at the same time. Mr Bingham's first fire took effect; it entered Mr O'Donel's left breast and pierced his heart.' He was killed without even having had a chance to return fire.

By the time of this incident, Denis Browne had built himself a house on the Erris estate inherited from his father. The site he chose was halfway down the peninsula, about nine miles south of the nearest town of note, Belmullet. The building faced north, across a naturally protected stretch of water called Elly Harbour. Architecturally it was highly ambitious, a five-bay house of two storeys, although the outer bay on each side rose a third storey. Single-storey wings on either side led to pavilions, one containing a conservatory, the other a chapel, so that the building in its entirety had a façade some 700 feet long. Although essentially a classical house, the whole building was covered in Gothic ornamentation so that it looked like a castle, complete with towers, turrets and a battlemented roofline. An early account of Bingham Castle is provided by writer John Bernard Trotter, who visited in October 1817, and whose account was published a year later. Travelling on horseback, it took him about an hour to reach the house from Carn, to the west of Belmullet. 'At some distance before us we perceived the very noble castle of Major Bingham. It is quite modern and scarcely finished, but has a very grand air, and highly ornaments so flat a country as this part of Erris. It is built in the old Gothic style, and its front extends a great way. The sea washes the borders of a handsome lawn; and the surrounding scenery of mountains, the island of Achill, and of the ocean, spreading on each side of the peninsula on which the castle stands, is quite unique and grand. The picturesque of the boldest kind.'

Duly impressed by his first view of the place, Trotter was delighted to note that

> the worthy possessor and founder of this noble pile, received us with the most genuine politeness, and shewed us the handsome apartments, and small elegant adjoining church of the castle, not yet finished. The interior of this building is adorned by many paintings; and a covered green-house connected with it will form, when finished, a pleasing winter walk in this exposed scite [sic]. Major B. had the goodness to shew us his farm and demesne, almost the whole of which he has, in the most praiseworthy manner, reclaimed and improved. The building of this castle must have given employment to great numbers, and still continues to do so.

Bingham Castle contained eleven bedrooms and four principal reception rooms. Of these, its last owner reported, the dining room 'possessed vaulted plaster ceilings, the work evidently of very good travelling craftsmen' while the main drawing room was 'characterised by oil paintings in the panelled ceiling'. Rose McCalmont cites an unnamed source reporting that the interior of Bingham Castle 'was ornamented with historical and allegorical paintings and the place has altogether a most imposing appearance'. It also contained many items relating to earlier generations of Binghams, since these had been bequeathed to Denis Bingham by his father. Of particular interest was a bowl traditionally used for family christenings. Rose McCalmont explained,

> the bowl is made of what is called delf ironstone, and the potter's name is G. Wooliscroft. In design, it may be noted, the bowl is eminently unecclesiastical, being decorated with flowers and a vase. The painting shows some influence of Oriental feeling, possibly Chinese, both in the colouring and the design. The bowl is not circular, as its edge is a dodecagon (twelve-sided). The ornamental border is in two halves, which reverse on either side, and these do not meet accurately. This border is apparently stamped on to the bowl. Round the outside there is a rather elegant conventional pattern. The diameter of the bowl is fifteen inches.

This, along with many other items once kept in the castle, was seemingly auctioned by Christie's in the mid-1960s.

Elsewhere on his estate, Major Bingham embarked on a programme of improvement. As engineer Patrick Knight reported in 1836, the major gave a number of his cotters 'each a piece to reclaim, rent free for a number of years (usually five); and, when the piece was reclaimed, the cotters were removed to the next unimproved part'. By this means, the improved parts of his property became 'by far the most productive part of the farm'.

Denis Bingham not only built himself a castle, but also a town further up the peninsula. John Bernard Trotter observed in 1817 that the owner of Bingham Castle 'thinks, I believe, of making a small market-town in some part of Erris. At present there is no post-office within from twenty to thirty miles of him or the other gentlemen of these parts.' A small settlement called Ballymacshedon already existed in the area, but this was now enlarged and renamed Binghamstown. Its developer entertained ambitious plans for the project, intending the town to become a centre for commerce. The challenges were immense, this part of the country then being even less developed than much of the west of Ireland, not least because of poor access; conducting a survey of County Mayo for the Dublin Society in 1801, James MacParlan called the roads around Erris 'completely bad and devious', while another in the vicinity he condemned as being 'a burlesque upon roads ... a satire upon the country'. Thirty years later, another report prepared for the Lord Lieutenant classified the region as consisting of 'vast tracts of boggy swamps, chiefly waste, interspersed with a few lakes and unculturable mountains'. Separated from the rest of Mayo by some thirty miles of inhospitable bog, the Erris region was scarcely accessible until well into the nineteenth century. Under these circumstances, establishing a new town and ensuring its commercial viability was no simple task; it was not until 1817 that a road was built between Castlebar and the Erris Peninsula, then extended by Denis Bingham to his own estates. The first two-wheeled vehicle was finally able to pass along it in early 1823. Extensive correspondence survives from this period between the owner of Bingham Castle and the Chief Secretary's office in Dublin. In June 1822, for example, the major wrote requesting the establishment of a scheme of public works such as the construction of the new road, since such an initiative was necessary for the poor of the area who were 'at Present, in an absolute state of Starvation and without a morsel of food, except what is supplied by the Fields or the Sea Shore'.

Bingham also sought to establish his new town as a fishing port, constructing a pier for this purpose and offering a local merchant 'A plot of one acre for building a house ... a lease for three lives rent free provided you would carry on the fishing business – If you will bring down a Company of six fishermen, I will give each of them, a small house built with one acre of Ground each Rent free during each of their lives provided they were always employed on the fishery ...'

Finally, and perhaps most importantly, in 1819 he received official permission to hold fairs and markets in Binghamstown four times annually. The venture looked set for success, but received a fatal setback in the mid-1820s when William Henry Carter, whose ancestor had married the younger daughter of Sir Arthur Shaen, decided to improve his own lands in Erris, not least by developing the town of Belmullet, which lies to the north of Binghamstown and through which the new road passed. Carter's intention was to establish 'a home market for produce that did not previously exist nearer than thirty miles by land'. Already in 1822 a coastguard station had been built here by the government. Three years later, Carter started to build a pier sufficiently large to accommodate vessels of 100 tons. He then applied to hold fairs in Belmullet.

Denis Bingham immediately lodged an objection with the authorities in Dublin, pointing out that he already had such a licence for Binghamstown and warning that should Carter receive permission to do likewise, the effect would be 'most materially injurious' to his town. His efforts were unsuccessful. Belmullet, which enjoyed the better and more convenient location, expanded rapidly. In 1823 it had contained only three decent houses; ten years later that number had risen to 185, with stores, shops and an hotel. Binghamstown correspondingly declined, with many of the town's schemes abandoned or not even begun. In Irish, the place's name is 'an Geata Mór', meaning The Big Gate. This is said to derive from a final attempt by Bingham to salvage his venture: in order to keep the Binghamstown fair going, he erected a large gate across the road and anyone who wished to pass through it to take livestock or other produce to the rival market at Belmullet was required to pay a toll. However, commercial forces were too strong. By the time Samuel Lewis visited Binghamstown for his *Topographical Dictionary of Ireland* (published 1837), while a monthly fair was still being held, the place, which he described as featuring 'one long street indifferently built', was in terminal decline. Two years later, in his *Tour in Connaught*, author and clergyman Caesar Otway called the town 'a monument to failure ... sinking fast into decay in consequence of its too great proximity to its younger sister, Belmullet'.

Denis Bingham died in 1842. While under the terms of his father's will he had been left 'the fee and inheritance of my Shaen estate', the same document warned that 'in case he dies without issue male my will is that it [the Shaen estate] reverts to my second son Henry Bingham, Esqre., and his right heirs for ever'. Denis Bingham had only one child, a daughter called Anne. To ensure that his line remained at Bingham Castle, in 1817 he arranged that she marry his brother Henry's son Robert Augustus Bingham. The marriage produced four children before Robert Augustus's accidental death eleven years later. According to Rose McCalmont, he was in the company of the editor and author of popular histories, Charles Knight. 'It was at the time when percussion-caps had just been introduced to supersede the flint-locks of firearms. Knight was showing Bingham how they were used on a pistol. The weapon went off, and Bingham was so badly wounded that he had only time to tell a hastily summoned servant that it was an accident before he died.'

When Denis Bingham in turn died in 1842 it was therefore his grandson, likewise called Denis, who at the age of twenty-five inherited the Bingham Castle estate. Three years later catastrophe overwhelmed this part of the country. Already suffering from want of investment and inadequate development, Mayo was one of the areas of Ireland worst affected by the Great Famine. Across the country, potatoes were the chief feature of the daily diet for approximately one-third of the population; in Mayo that figure rose to nine-tenths. The blight that destroyed this staple foodstuff therefore had devastating consequences, not least on the economically and agriculturally backward Erris peninsula. Writing in March 1847 the English Quaker William Bennett who had come to the region so that he could report back to his co-religious, described it as 'one of the most remote and destitute corners ... the scenes of human misery and degradation we witnessed still haunt my imagination, with the vividness and power of some horrid and tyrannous delusion, rather than the features of a sober reality'.

By this time, with the late major's plans for a new town long since abandoned, Binghamstown had sunk into a state of wretchedness, as a number of visitors to the area commented. The consequences of the famine were as bad here as everywhere else in Mayo, with large numbers of people dying either of starvation or disease, and others leaving, never to return. In the early 1830s, once it became clear the advance of Belmullet could not be halted and the Binghams lost hope in making Binghamstown a success, they had let the town and surrounding land to a man called Luke Lyons. His brother, Dean John Patrick Lyons, a Roman Catholic priest, rented Binghamstown House, built by Major Bingham as part of the original development, and by far its most substantial residence. During the years of famine, Luke Lyons engaged in a brutal policy of clearing the town's buildings; when philanthropist James Hack Tuke saw the place in February 1847, he counted at least thirty roofless houses. It has been estimated that Luke Lyons was one of the worst evictors during this terrible period. In March 1848 Richard Hamilton, appointed the previous autumn as Poor Law Inspector at Belmullet, reported to the Dublin government that Lyons had 'removed nearly all the occupying tenants holding under him. I understand Mr Lyons is a wealthy man, but I believe he does not purpose cultivating his lands this year.' As for the Binghams of Bingham Castle, he wrote, 'Their arable lands are generally waste; they have no means to cultivate them.' In consequence, when towards the end of the decade the years of famine drew to a close, Binghamstown, which had already been in decline, grew steadily more impoverished.

In her *Letters from Ireland* (1852) English author Harriet Martineau described the place as

> the most shocking wreck we have seen, except perhaps one other village in another part of Mayo. We found more inhabitants remaining than we had expected, and they did not look personally miserable at all. But the lines of ruin where there was once a street, the weeds and filth about the deserted hearthstones, or (what seemed almost worse), the crops of potatoes and cabbages grown on the floors where dead neighbours lived so lately, made our very hearts sick.

A decade later, another visitor to the region, Henry Coulter, thought Binghamstown 'one of the most decayed, poverty-stricken places in appearance that I have ever seen'. It would never recover.

Like many other landowners in the west of Ireland, Denis Bingham found himself in straitened circumstances and forced to turn to the Encumbered Estates Court, an agency established by legislation in 1849 to take over estates from heavily indebted owners and sell them, the proceeds then being distributed among creditors. In 1854 almost 13,000 acres of Denis Bingham's land were offered for sale through the court, and more followed the next year. In addition, land inherited by his wife Elizabeth Nash had been sold by the court in 1853. Married in February 1846 she was the only child and heiress of Arthur Nash of Carne, an estate on the peninsula north of Belmullet, and her inheritance helped to keep the family in residence at Bingham Castle, unlike many other landowners who were forced to sell everything; in 1876 Denis Bingham still owned 4827 acres in the county.

The couple had six children, their eldest son and heir, born in 1849, being another Denis Bingham. He married in 1874 but died just two years later, leaving two infant sons. Thus, when the older Denis died in 1902, Bingham Castle was once more inherited by a grandson, again called Denis and the last of the family to live in the house. Then in his mid-twenties, on coming into possession of the estate, he found it had been heavily mortgaged by his grandfather and was in imminent danger of foreclosure. 'I worked hard & cleared off all the mortgages,' he wrote later. 'In fact, I cleared off the last one in 1921.' As for Bingham Castle, 'It was originally in bad repair. I spent all my time renovating it and had it in first class order.' He estimated his expenditure on the house over these years to have been in the region of £1200.

In 1909 he married a first cousin (as had his great-grandfather almost a century earlier), Ina Broad, whose father Captain George Broad had been Master of Queen Victoria's yacht, the *Alberta*. Denis Bingham's cousin Theresa Bingham-Daly wrote that the couple inherited many items once on the yacht, including a number of paintings of the vessel, the maple chair used by Victoria when sitting on deck, and among a large collection of tableware, 'two decanters; twenty-six drinking glasses; a jam dish with cover; approximately one hundred pieces of porcelain from services used on the Royal yachts and at Osborne'. These were all kept at Bingham Castle until the mid-1920s, and later donated by Denis and Ina Bingham to the National Maritime Museum, Greenwich where they remain.

According to Theresa Bingham-Daly, Ina Broad was something of an heiress, which may have helped clear some of the debts her husband inherited. Her money allowed him to invest in a large walled garden where 'Denis's pride and joy was his magnificent green house, glowing with strawberries, raspberries, tomatoes, peppers, cucumbers and some exotic fruits. Any surplus was bottled for winter. The orchard produced apples, pears, red plums, golden plums, greengages, gooseberries, black currants and blackberries.'

Following the outbreak of hostilities between Britain and Germany in 1914, Denis Bingham, by then aged almost forty, volunteered and received a commission as a lieutenant in the Royal Naval Volunteer Reserve '& did anything I could, principally coast watching – unpaid and I supplied all my own uniform'. He also assisted with recruiting

Irishmen to join the armed forces and, looking back many years later, concluded this was the main reason 'I had such a bad time during 1922 & 1923.'

The bad time began, as was often the case, with minor irritants to daily life. Denis Bingham appears to have got through the years of the War of Independence without damage to his property, although he experienced sufficient intimidation that in 1921 he tried to sell Bingham Castle and an adjacent 260 acres of land through a Dublin agent. Given the circumstances, no offers were forthcoming, although he did manage to let the place on several occasions for £40 a month, but 'owing to the troubles I am not able to let or sell it at any price'.

Those troubles began in earnest on the evening of 13 April 1922 when a group of more than fifty armed men came to the house and demanded that Denis Bingham hand over one of his farms. 'I offered to sell them the farm or alternatively I would reserve the grazing for my own tenants, as I had done for the 10 or 11 years previously.' The men's response was to warn he would be boycotted, after which they 'went up to one of my fields and took the 5 men that were working for me away. They then went to the back door and warned my two servants to clear out of the house within 3 days. The maids left on morning of the 15th inst.'

A week later, in the early hours of 20 April, shots were fired over the house occupied by the Bingham herdsman who was then taken from his bed by a group of men, beaten and left in a drain. 'This man displayed great loyalty to me, but was threatened with his life and had to leave ...' The following day six armed men entered the Bingham Castle coachhouse and removed the owner's car, a Citroen which he had bought the previous July for £382; it was returned a fortnight later 'in a damaged condition' and then stolen again in late June, being restored to him at the start of August even more damaged than before, 'hood broken to bits ... glass & lamps all gone, wings broken, springs broken, several other parts broken & wheels fastened with cart bolts'.

Meanwhile, fences and walls were destroyed and large numbers of livestock driven to graze on his land, and later in the autumn considerable quantities of his own cattle and sheep were stolen. He had already tried to sell some of the former, but could find no buyer locally, so had to drive them fifty miles across the county to a market in Ballina where he was not known; 'There were men on watch day & night to see no one came to help me & I had no one all that time to mind 60 cattle, 2 horses, 5 cows and several calves.'

By now, only Denis Bingham, his wife and her elderly mother were living in the house. They were raided for the first time on the evening of 30 April 1922 when some forty men turned up demanding arms, threatening to search the building if nothing was given to them; a gun and a revolver, together with some cartridges, were handed over. Almost three weeks later, another group of men arrived at the house and even though he had given what arms had been on the premises, this time they insisted on searching for themselves, revolvers being held to the heads of Denis Bingham and his wife. Later the family discovered the men had 'actually gone about the house with a hatchet & damaged some of the furniture & chipped the mahogany banisters. They forced lids of trunks, pulled boxes about, damaged lacquer boxes, burst hinges …' Money and jewellery were stolen, and large numbers of work tools taken from outhouses. Over the winter months more raids on the land and livestock occurred, more goods were taken and then on 1 January 1923 Denis Bingham woke to see his two ricks of hay on fire, the blaze entirely destroying them.

As the year progressed and they faced an ongoing boycott from the local community, it became increasingly difficult for the Binghams to envisage remaining in their home. They began to consider leaving not just Bingham Castle and Mayo, but Ireland. No longer able to farm, and unable to sell the house or surrounding land owing to the boycott, they thought to raise at least some money on which to live by selling many of Bingham Castle's contents. However, the local IRA warned potential buyers to stay away, and, having been postponed for twenty-four hours the event was a failure with the items that did sell going for pathetically low sums. A cupboard, for example, judged to be worth £20 went for just £1 and six shillings. An oak table fetched just £4, its accompanying four chairs £2, and these were among the auction's best prices, since most lots went for a matter of shillings. A Grandfather clock was sold for £4 and ten shillings, as was an old mahogany bed, the latter's accompanying dressing table making £5 and five shillings. Sets of books went for a couple of shillings, a Wedgwood china service for eight shillings, a pair of curtains and their poles for twelve shillings. Among the farm implements, typically ten shillings was paid for a chain harrow, recently bought for £6 and ten shillings, and eight shillings for a portable poultry house (never used, also bought for £6 and ten shillings). And so it humiliatingly crept on until someone paid three shillings for the final lot, simply described as a 'set of ornaments'. The auctioneer sent in his bill. In total the sale – which had been expected to make in the region of £850 – realized just £292, ten shillings and twopence. When deductions were made for advertising, bill posting and various other costs (including 'Groceries, £2.10.0'), the Binghams received a cheque for £276, fourteen shillings and eightpence, deemed to be the value of their former possessions.

At the start of 1924 Denis Bingham reluctantly made the decision to leave Ireland: 'As a result of all this treatment, my nerves suffered and also my wife's & I have become slightly deaf.' Together with her mother – who would die just a few months later – they moved to England, spending some £2000 to buy a house in Broadstone, a village just a few miles from Poole in Dorset. They named the place Newbrook, a memory of the Bingham house in Mayo whence his branch of the family had come. It was, of course, considerably smaller than their previous home, but certainly much safer. Denis Bingham now embarked on applying to the Irish Grants Committee for compensation, explaining in a covering letter: 'I was one of what was termed the Landlord class. I lived among my tenants for 33 1/2 years and had my home there.' The eventual sum sought in compensation was £23,065. This included £15,250 for loss of capital value of the house and lands and £1793 for loss of profits on the lands they had hitherto farmed, as well as other items such as £194 for loss on the forced sale of cattle, and £60 for turf looted. Finally in March 1929 the Binghams were informed that they would be awarded £5490.

Back in Ireland, Bingham Castle was left standing empty. As Denis Bingham explained, 'When I left I tried to sell it and have failed. It is now rapidly falling into ruins. It is impossible to sell or let it.' As a result, the Land Commission announced that it would compulsorily purchase the land around the building to be divided into small holdings and paying its owner £1700, which he deemed 'a very small sum, no value being put upon the house as it is of course useless for their purpose'. Unlike many other similar properties, Bingham Castle was not burnt out nor demolished. Instead, it was simply abandoned and left to fall down. Today the site where the building once stood is demarcated only by a few low stone walls on the edge.

3

'A House that had been occupied as a residence for several hundred years'
ARDFERT, COUNTY KERRY

HOUSES IN THE Dublin suburb of Glenageary are much sought-after today, not least on affluent Marlborough Road where in 2019 one property was put on the market for €2.9 million. However, it is unlikely that residents on this street realize the majority of their homes only came to be built a century ago as the result of another house being destroyed on the other side of the country, in County Kerry.

To understand how this came about, it is necessary to go back almost 400 years and across to the Irish Midlands where, in the 1550s, England's Queen Mary embarked on a policy of planting loyal settlers from her own country. To assist this process she created Queen's County and King's County, now known as Laois and Offaly, but then named after herself and her husband, Philip II of Spain. Threatened with dispossession, most Irish families long settled in this part of the country fought back, but a few pragmatically opted to support English government policy, recognizing here an opportunity to improve their own circumstances. Among those who chose this recourse were two brothers, Pádraic and Sean Mac an Chrosáin, whose forebears had served as hereditary bards to the O'Moores, the dominant clan in what is now County Laois. The Mac an Chrosáin siblings soon anglicized their names to become Patrick and John Crosbie, and declared loyalty to the Crown.

Patrick, employed for many years as an administrator by the government, was duly rewarded with grants of land in his own part of the country, even as other long-standing occupants were having their property bestowed on the new settlers. However, in addition and often by dubious means, he also managed to acquire substantial acreage in north Kerry where, by the mid-1580s and in the aftermath of the failed Desmond Rebellions, a policy of settlement was similarly being implemented. Meanwhile John Crosbie became an Anglican clergyman and, being as diligent a supporter of the official regime as Patrick, quickly rose through church ranks until in 1601 he was appointed Bishop of Ardfert and Aghadoe, a position he held for the next twenty years. During this time, once more like his brother, he took full advantage of every opportunity to acquire land, not least because he had to provide for the future of his seven sons (he and his wife Winifred also had six daughters for whom provision needed to be made).

It was the second of these sons, David Crosbie, whose descendants would remain at Ardfert until the 1920s. They chose to take up residence adjacent to an old Franciscan friary on the outskirts of the town, founded in 1253 by Thomas FitzMaurice who is supposed to have been buried on the site when he died a few years later. The friary underwent various upheavals but survived until the closure of all such houses in the second half of the sixteenth century, after which an English soldier, John Zouche, turned the buildings into a barracks. But then it passed into the hands of David Crosbie who in the second quarter of the seventeenth century decided to build himself a new residence next to the friary. Over its entrance, he placed a stone carrying the inscription: 'Hoc Opus Incaeptum A.D. 1633 Et Finitum A.D. 1635, David Crosbie Armiger, Ubi Fides et Veritas Deus Providebit'. No doubt he thought this fine house would stand long into the future, but early in the course of the Confederate Wars of the following decade it was entirely swept away. (The inscribed stone, long thought lost, was rediscovered in the mid-nineteenth century built into a gate pier and once more placed over the house's entrance, only to be lost again in 1921).

At some date towards the end of the seventeenth century David Crosbie's son Thomas built another house, once more adjacent to the old Franciscan ruins. Although it would come to be considered hopelessly old-fashioned, at the time of its construction Ardfert Abbey represented the height of architectural good taste. The main block ran to seven bays and two storeys, the central breakfront crowned by a tall pediment. This building was flanked by short wings, which soon turned at right angles to project forward and create a substantial forecourt, ensuring an impressive arrival for visitors. Around the house, the grounds were laid out with formal gardens, terraced to the rear, and featuring yew alleys and long avenues of beech, lime and elm. Inside, the reception rooms were panelled, with the entrance hall being further decorated at some unknown date in the eighteenth century when near life-size grisaille figures in classical garb were painted on the walls. Beyond this room lay the main staircase, the steps wide and shallow as was then fashionable, and with each baluster carved to look like a fluted Corinthian column.

Thomas Crosbie's grandson Maurice carried out further works at Ardfert Abbey in the 1720s but he also improved his family's circumstances, both by marrying Lady Anne FitzMaurice, daughter of the first Earl of Kerry, and then by acquiring a title of his own, becoming a knight in 1711 and finally Baron Branden in 1758. During the previous decade, his heir William had married Lady Theodosia Bligh, daughter of the Earl of Darnley, and brought her to Ardfert, which she had never seen before. The journey to what was then a remote part of Kerry was not without its travails, the newly-weds much troubled by fleas, although in Limerick city they were greeted by the army, bells were rung in their honour, and they were given dinner by a local wine merchant and his wife.

Finally they reached their destination, at which point the bride burst into tears despite the warm welcome extended by her new parents-in-law. However, as she later wrote to her sister Lady Mary Tighe, 'I was in pucker enough all dinner time. But I assure you that before we went to bed I was so great with Lady Anne as if I'd been acquainted with her all my life.' The following morning she was presented with a purse of one hundred guineas and told to buy herself something at a local fair; her husband then promised a further fifty guineas.

Inevitably, the couple attracted many visitors eager to meet William's new wife. Some she welcomed, others she described as 'locusts', writing again to her sister of 'an old, rusty, grunting Bishop' who came to stay at Ardfert Abbey for a fortnight but being feeble, 'he can't walk about with the men and so is left upon our hands the whole day long, and a heavy load he is. God knows, I shall never endure the sight of a black gown again, for there is such a regiment here of them, every day, dancing attendance after him, that it quite kills me.' Other visitors only came for a few hours, such as a Colonel Ponsonby who arrived with his wife and sister-in-law. Unfortunately Lady Theodosia took against these women, who turned up in 'their best Castle gowns'. It transpired that they had sent for a maid to dress them in this fashion: 'This I heard the day before they came and it gave me a strong prejudice against them.'

Life at Ardfert appears to have been intensely social, with lots of picnics and outings in the locality, as well as gatherings on the local strand, although these met with less favour since Lady Theodosia reported, 'they seldom end till every man is completely drunk, but such things must be, at this time, to please the higher power'. The family then decamped for a week to Dingle where there were balls every night, and boating and racing during the day.

After more than thirty years of marriage and five children, Lady Theodosia died in May 1777, just ten months after her husband had been created Earl of Glandore. He in turn would die in April 1781, when the couple's only surviving son, John, inherited title and estate. Then based in London, for a time it appeared as though the heir would not return to Kerry. A few months after his mother's death, he had married the Hon. Diana Sackville, a daughter of Lord George Germain, now remembered for being a somewhat hapless Secretary of State for the American Department during the American War of Independence. According to Lady Louisa Stuart, prior to her marriage, Lady Diana had been 'conceited and disagreeable, a sort of *pattern* Miss who lectured us all upon propriety'. But soon after being wed, her character underwent a transformation, and she became 'a most dissipated, fine lady, flirting, gaming, etc., beyond her fellows'. As far as Lady Louisa was concerned, the new Lady Glandore was just 'unusually silly'. Of greater concern was her tardiness in paying gambling debts, for which she was given the nickname 'Owen Glendower' (pronounced 'Owing Glandore').

As for her husband, Lady Louisa Stuart was similarly dismissive, calling him 'a strange, absent, staring sort of being'. She told how, invited by his wife's cousin the Duke of Dorset to shoot at Knole, Lord Glandore 'fell into a reverie, took aim, and very quietly shot a pointer instead of a partridge. The sportsmen, not knowing what might happen next, made the best of their way home, and never invited him to go a-shooting again.' It may be because both of them had blotted their respective copybooks that some two years after coming into his inheritance, Lord Glandore finally brought his wife to live at Ardfert. And there they remained, swapping the smart society of London and Dublin for that to be found in Tralee, where at a ball in the Assembly Rooms, officially opened 'in all the glory of diamonds, pointed lace, powder and brocade' by Lady Glandore, she would graciously walk about the room between dances, 'smiling and chatting with many of the town and country gentry like a veritable grand dame'.

Nevertheless, she must have found it a tedious existence, not least because Ardfert Abbey, once so fashionable in its design, was now hopelessly out of step with more recent architectural trends. When the Reverend Daniel Beaufort, himself a talented amateur architect, visited the place in 1788 he described it as 'extremely low, ill-contrived and ugly, the furniture mean and the prospect bad. In the gardens are some shady walks, clipt arcades, weeping willows in abundance – and everything inspires la melancholie to which the ruin of a large fine Abbey contributes its share.'

His opinion of Ardfert Abbey was shared by Caroline, Countess of Portarlington, who with her husband had three years earlier spent a few days staying with the Glandores. The Portarlingtons experienced almost as dreadful a journey to Kerry as had Lady Theodosia back in 1745, once again discovering en route 'fleas enough to devour us'. They arrived to a warm welcome at Ardfert, their host and hostess 'very glad to see a new face, for tho' there are several people in the house with them, yet their neighbourhood is thin, and she has been here these two years without stirring, which, to be sure, is doing penance for a young woman that likes diversions as much as she does'. Furthermore, as far as Lady Portarlington was concerned, the Glandores' home was 'a dismal place, and he is so partial to everything that is old that he is determined not to alter it'. The interior was filled 'with small low rooms, wainscotted, and the drawing room perfectly antique, which he won't let her alter. It is with difficulty he has let her fit up a little dressing room belonging to the apartment I am in, which indeed she has made a sweet little place.'

As for Lady Glandore, far from being the 'unusually silly' woman recalled by Lady Louisa Stuart, she appeared to be far more pleasant than expected, 'and the people here seem to admire her very much'. All went well with the visit until one evening the post arrived, with a letter advising that Lady Glandore's father had died, which threw a pall over the occasion and encouraged the Portarlingtons to take their leave of Kerry. They never returned and nor does Ardfert, still so remote since roads were poor, appear to have attracted many other visitors. By the time Thomas Barnard, Bishop of Limerick, came to stay in 1799, he would write that the household was 'one of the most regular and best-conducted that I have ever seen in Ireland' with guests encouraged to read in the library before everyone retired early to bed. During his visit the bishop observed not 'a shadow of gaming', suggesting that Lady Glandore no longer gambled, and no 'soaking' by which he meant heavy drinking. Other evidence suggests Ardfert's chatelaine was fond of alcohol, even if she refrained from its consumption in front of her clerical guests. Beer appears to have been her beverage of choice, and preferably brewed in England, since she wrote regularly to a family friend there asking that he send over fresh supplies: 'I cannot drink the beer at my own house and it is quite a misfortune to me.' Not long afterwards, she wrote again: 'It is a long time since you have thought of replenishing this old Mansion with comfortable strong Beer, you know my brother always allows me a large cask to be sent to me yearly, and I cannot suffer you to forget it, pray send it off as soon as you can, for we have not a single drop left.' Lady Glandore's beer consumption appears to have had consequences for her health because when another friend, Justice Robert Day, visited Ardfert in September 1811, he did not see his hostess as she was confined to bed with gout, 'though she denies it'.

Two years earlier Judge Day had attempted to secure a well-paid office for Lord Glandore, an indication that the latter's expenditure now exceeded his income, with unhappy consequences for any future owner of the estate. The position of second Postmaster General of Ireland was sought, and although the Duke of Richmond, then Lord Lieutenant, seemed favourable to the idea and indeed spent two nights at Ardfert Abbey while on a tour of Kerry in September 1809, eventually the second Earl of Rosse was awarded the role. Having never held any public office before, Lord Glandore's chances of being given one now, when he was in his mid-fifties, were always going to be slim.

He died in October 1815, his wife having predeceased him by fourteen months. The Glandores had three children but all died soon after birth, which may explain why she at one point had opened a boarding school in the village. On his death, the earldom lapsed but the title of Baron Branden passed to a cousin, William Crosbie, a Church of Ireland clergyman. Aged forty-four, he had recently married the much younger Elizabeth La Touche, but the union was not a success and before long the couple separated. In spring 1828 the English politician and inveterate gossip Thomas Creevey recorded in his journal that

Lord Branden, who is a divine as well as a peer, got possession of a correspondence between his lady and Mr. Secretary Lamb [the future Lord Melbourne, who at the time was serving as Secretary of State for Ireland] which left no doubt to him or anyone else, as to the nature of the connection between these young people; so he writes a letter to the lady announcing his discovery, but he adds if she will exert her interest with Mr. Lamb to procure him a Bishopric, he will overlook her offence, and restore her the letters; to which my lady replies, she shall neither degrade herself nor Mr. Lamb by making any such application, but that she is very grateful to my lord for the letter he has written her, which she shall put immediately into Mr. Lamb's possession.

Lord Branden subsequently brought an action against Lamb for Criminal Conversation (in effect, adultery). The case was thrown out of court, but it was always believed the clergyman had been bought off by Lamb; in any case, Lord Branden retired to Nice where he died in comfort in 1832. His widow, left with a tarnished reputation, would survive another thirty years.

As for the Ardfert estate, it was bequeathed to another Anglican clergyman, John Talbot, whose mother Lady Anne Crosbie had been one of the second Lord Glandore's sisters. Within a few months of his uncle's death, the heir had legally changed his surname to Talbot-Crosbie. However, he did not have long to enjoy his inheritance, dying in January 1818 and leaving behind a son, William, born only ten months earlier. A brother, John, was born eight months after their father's death.

The two boys, and their two elder sisters Anne and Diana, were brought up by their widowed mother, with a pair of uncles acting as the children's legal guardians. One of those uncles, William Talbot, lived at Mount Talbot, County Roscommon, and having no children of his own he proposed to leave his estate to his nephew and namesake, William Talbot-Crosbie, provided the latter leave his studies at Trinity

College Cambridge and enter a cavalry regiment. The other condition was that the Ardfert estate, by then much neglected and in debt, be sold. Perhaps because they had no children and were therefore less concerned about the future than might otherwise have been the case, the Glandores had lived well beyond their means, leaving the estate so heavily indebted that income scarcely covered financial obligations. It is understandable that the best solution seemed to be a sale of the property. Nevertheless, the mother of Mount Talbot's putative heir resisted the idea that Ardfert be sold and, no commission into a regiment materializing, it remained in the hands of William Talbot-Crosbie. (Mount Talbot would in due course be inherited by his younger brother John.)

Ardfert's unhappy state became apparent to its owner, even before he came of age, when he began to spend time on the property. Left unoccupied for many years, in the main building, 'the staircase, the floor of the library and the floor of the hall were all rotten. In fact, the whole house had to be gutted and restored. Of the kitchen wing, only the walls remained, the roof, floor and windows were all rotten and required renewal.' The old stable wing likewise had to be re-roofed, as soon as funds permitted, with new accommodation for servants and another kitchen following in due course. By now, William Talbot-Crosbie had married Susan Burrell, with whom he would have seven children before she died in 1850, after which he married her sister Emma (and following her death he married again, this time to a widow).

Not just the main house, but other buildings throughout the estate were similarly improved or rebuilt, giving tenants better accommodation than the cabins of mud and thatch they had hitherto occupied. Substantial drainage works took place, increasing the amount of agricultural land available, new roads were created, and the local river embanked, thereby reducing the likelihood of flooding. In the second half of the nineteenth century the Ardfert estate became famous for the quality of its Shorthorn herd, annual sales of young bulls being held there each spring from 1852 onwards. Those attending this event, some of whom had come from as far away as South America, would be provided with lunch in the granary before the auction got underway. Talbot-Crosbie's improvements meant that by 1874 *The Farmer's Magazine* could write, 'Absentee landlords might take a profitable lesson from the good example set at Ardfert, where comfort, order and prosperity reign.'

Many years later Ardfert's owner declared that had he not taken personal control of the estate early and put it on a sound financial footing, he would have been ruined during the years of the Great Famine. But in the aftermath of that terrible period, from the late 1850s onwards, he became ever more preoccupied with generating as much income as possible. Having inherited a heavily indebted property, and now, in the post-famine period, seeing so many of his fellow landlords obliged to sell their estates, he sought to avoid facing the same fate. Between 1855 and 1877 rents charged to Ardfert's tenants steadily increased, overall by two-thirds of their previous figure. While these additional sums could usually be paid during the earlier period, the long agricultural slump that began in the 1870s left many tenants unable to meet their obligations. The absence of fixity of tenure, not just here but throughout the country, left them haunted by fear of eviction, which for some at least now became a reality. In the 1860s Talbot-Crosbie embarked on a policy of land clearance so as to make parts of the estate more financially efficient. In addition, he sought to extend the demesne boundaries to take in more of Ardfert village, including the medieval cathedral and its graveyard. This involved the demolition of many houses, earning him the sobriquet by which he is still remembered in the area: Billy the Leveller. His efforts to close an ancient road to the cathedral and replace it with a new one were fiercely resisted by the local people, led by their parish priest. In consequence of these actions, much of the good he had done in the area and the improvements he had carried out were forgotten, and only his more recent behaviour remembered. By 1881 a writer in the *Kerry Evening Post* could refer to him as 'The

Attila of North Kerry, a very merciless landlord who has blotted out the ancient city of Ardfert.'

William Talbot-Crosbie's actions seem strange given his passionately held religious convictions: he was another of the County Kerry landlords who had left the Church of Ireland to become a member of the Plymouth Brethren. At Ardfert, he converted one of the outbuildings into a chapel, so that followers of the sect might have a place to meet. In 1870 actor-turned-preacher John Hambleton wrote

> I went to see Mr. Crosbie ... The butler (Fidler his name) and all the servants were happy and rejoicing Christians and becoming real labourers in the vineyard. In the evening we held a meeting in the loft, and upwards of 100 converts with open Bibles listened to the expounding of the Word; and such a time of refreshing we had that it seemed Heaven had come down to earth. Every Protestant in this village seemed converted to God.

Every Protestant perhaps, but the local Roman Catholic population, most of whom were his tenants, proved less easy to win over. Despite Talbot-Crosbie's best efforts the Plymouth Brethren remained in a minority around Ardfert.

Long before his death in September 1899, trouble had broken out on the estate. Due to the many changes he had instigated in its management, the place was now much more profitable than had been the case previously, not least thanks to higher rents paid by tenants. Following the onset of the Land Wars in the early 1880s, reductions in these were sought – and won, much to Talbot-Crosbie's chagrin. The passage of successive government Land Acts from 1870 made rent reduction inevitable, with consequences for the incomes of all estate owners. At Ardfert Abbey, the family estimated that the annual revenue from rental had grown from £3126 in 1839 (soon after William Talbot-Crosbie had come of age and taken over responsibility for the estate) to £8421 in 1879, after which it began to decline, dropping before the end of the century to £5321, a drop of 20 per cent. As far as its owners were concerned, the effect 'was to render the estate practically insolvent'.

This was the state of affairs when William Talbot-Crosbie died at the age of eighty-two. Ardfert Abbey was inherited by his eldest son John who, following a long illness, died just two months later. The estate now passed to the second son, Lindsey, whose conciliatory approach to ongoing conflicts in Ireland between landlord and tenant was in stark contrast to the immutable antagonism displayed by his late father. Until then, the Irish Landowners' Convention, established in 1886, had represented the interests of their class. The convention was inherently conservative and resistant to any change in land ownership, inclined to resist all government efforts to achieve a solution to this seemingly intractable problem. Tenant representatives, led by the United Irish League, were equally determined not to give ground on their demand that agricultural land be compulsorily purchased from landlords for distribution among their members. With neither side prepared to yield, the situation appeared hopeless.

Then in the spring of 1902 a series of letters was published in Irish newspapers, all written by Lindsey Talbot-Crosbie, who described himself as an 'emancipated landlord'. Demonstrating the truth of this description, his correspondence consistently called for a round-table conference of tenant and landlord representatives. 'Has not the time arrived,' he suggested in the *Irish Independent*, 'when an attempt should be made by moderate men of different parties to ascertain their points of agreement and endeavour to seek some course that will bring peace to our distracted country?' Furthermore, he was prepared to do more than merely publish a proposal: 'As a beginning must be made somewhere, I shall be glad to receive communications from those who may be prepared to render assistance in bringing this about.' Communications soon followed, from all sides and opinions, and a path to reconciliation was found, leading to the Land Conference of December 1902 and eventually to the following year's

Land Purchase (Ireland) Act, commonly called the Wyndham Act after George Wyndham, then Chief Secretary for Ireland who steered the legislation to successful conclusion. Yet without Lindsey Talbot-Crosbie's initiative, one that risked putting him at odds with his fellow landlords, the act might never have come into being. He took the first step that led to a fundamental change in land ownership in Ireland, facilitating the transfer of some nine million acres even by 1914. Some of that had, until then, formed the Ardfert Abbey estate: this was now sold to tenants, with the Talbot-Crosbies retaining, under the terms of the Wyndham Act's buy-back scheme, only the 528-acre demesne around the house.

In the aftermath Lindsey Talbot-Crosbie turned his attention more directly to politics, working with the Earl of Dunraven to establish a new organization, the Irish Reform Association, which championed the idea of moderate devolution. The attempt to win support for such an idea provoked violent opposition, especially among unionists in Ulster, and following a political crisis in 1905, the association faded from view. As political positions hardened over the years running up to the First World War, Talbot-Crosbie appears to have grown increasingly in favour of Home Rule. Following his unexpected death in November 1913, the nationalist *Kerry Sentinel* declared: 'Not only through this county did his public actions make him influential and popular to a marked degree, but his vigorous letters to the London and Irish press contributed in no small measure to the success of the Irish demand for self-government.'

His original heir Hugh having died of wounds in the Boer War in 1901, what remained of the estate was now once again inherited by a younger son, although not, as might have been expected, the next in line. This was John Burrell Talbot-Crosbie who, according to family lore, was disinherited because he had married without his parents' approval. He does not appear to have let this setback affect him, becoming a successful industrialist in Scotland, chairman of sugar machinery manufacturers Duncan Stewart & Co. as well as sitting on the board of the British Sugar Corporation and at one time owning a 25 per cent stake in Rangers Football Club.

Ardfert meanwhile passed to the next brother, Edward Wynne Talbot-Crosbie, always known in the family as Wynne. Like his elder sibling, he was based in Scotland so the house continued to be occupied by their mother Anne. She was still living there when the First World War ended, but by December 1919, with the War of Independence under way and the local Royal Irish Constabulary barracks closed the previous month (it would be burnt down the following April), she no longer felt safe at Ardfert. Leaving the domestic staff still in the house, she moved to Dublin, initially staying in a hotel before renting a furnished house. By then in her mid-seventies, her intention was to return to Ardfert once local conditions made this possible. Meanwhile, despite the presence of staff, the family's absence from Ardfert Abbey encouraged various attacks on the demesne, with trees cut down, gates and palings stolen, and walls knocked. Between April 1920 and May 1921, compensation was awarded no less than eight times for damage done to the property, with the house itself damaged on at least one occasion.

By September 1921, having found large numbers of items removed from outbuildings, the Talbot-Crosbies were no longer confident that the main building's contents were safe. They arranged to have the most important pieces of furniture and paintings removed, in thirteen vans, and shipped to Chester where Anne Talbot-Crosbie had then taken up residence (and where she would die in April 1928). But having no income on which to live, she and her son reached the decision that their only option was to sell these heirlooms, offering them for sale through the local auctioneer, Brown's of Chester, in mid-December 1921.

The catalogue lists almost two hundred lots, of varying quality: several pairs of lined and padded silk curtains, for example, as well as eight yards of Axminster stair carpet in three pieces and the usual brass fenders, bedroom wardrobes, washstands and so forth. But other items were of considerable importance, such as an eighteenth-century mahogany pedestal desk, originally owned by the second Earl of Glandore. According to a note in a surviving catalogue, this was sold to the Cunard shipping company. Then there was a Louis XV boulle-and-tortoiseshell table, and a considerable selection of French Empire tables and pier glasses, many with ormolu mounts. In this instance, the valuable contents of Ardfert Abbey were lost not through fire or theft but due to financial necessity. Less important goods left behind in Kerry were offered for auction, realizing £700. As a further financial saving, the domestic staff were now paid off and just a caretaker retained. The decision to empty the house and close it up would soon cause difficulties for the family.

Following the onset of the Civil War, Ardfert Abbey was occupied between April and May 1922 by the Irregulars (members of the anti-Treaty force) and it may have been during this period that a number of fittings were stolen since two local men were later charged for having items such as a marble chimney piece in their possession. Even before then, another house on the demesne called Annadale, together with the pump yard, were attacked 'and a quantity of doors, windows and other property ... were wantonly and maliciously broken'. The situation grew steadily worse. Finally, on 3 August 1922, Ardfert Abbey was set on fire and completely gutted, as was Abbeylands, a rectory owned by the family.

A claim for compensation was duly lodged, initially for £100,000, a sum so large it seems to have been selected at random. By October 1922 the figure had dropped to £50,000. When the claim was finally lodged, the eventual amount sought was £23,464, four shillings and threepence. Far from being excessive, this now looks a very modest sum, but when the matter came before a judge in Listowel, County Kerry, in May 1924, the State Solicitor argued that since the house's furniture had been removed, and no one was living in the property at the time of the fire, it could not be deemed the family's residence. Furthermore, he insisted, the market price of the building was only

£2200, no value being placed on its historical worth. The court agreed with these arguments, and the Talbot-Crosbies were accordingly awarded just £2250 for the loss of Ardfert Abbey, this amount being conditional on a partial reconstruction of the house. (A further £900 was granted for the destruction of Abbeylands, and £200 for the loss of items in the stable block.)

Understandably, the family appealed this decision, Wynne Talbot-Crosbie writing directly to the Free State's then-president William T. Cosgrave, pointing out that only nine months had passed between the removal of furniture and destruction of house,

> and it seems to me a departure from the spirit of the Compensation Act to contend that after a house that had been occupied as a residence for several hundred years and would have continued to be my mother's residence except for the disturbed conditions of the country, that it ceased to be a residence because she was not residing in it, and the furniture had been removed.

Cosgrave sent back a tactful response explaining that he had looked into the matter, but could obviously not interfere in a judicial decision, and moreover, since the Talbot-Crosbies had lodged an appeal against that decision, 'the most satisfactory course for you would be to allow the appeal to proceed'.

Proceed it duly did, and this time much more to the family's satisfaction: in September 1925 a judge in Dublin awarded the Talbot-Crosbies £21,024. The partial reconstruction condition remained in place, meaning the beneficiaries could not simply take the money and spend it as they wished. In this instance, however, a clause in the award allowed them an alternative option. By now, given what had been done to their property, the family had no desire to return to Ardfert. Wynne Talbot-Crosbie was settled in Scotland, his mother in England: the long-standing link with County Kerry, going back to the sixteenth century, had been irreparably broken. However, as was noted in press reports of the appeal court judgement, the reconstruction clause simply stipulated that 'the amount of the compensation must be spent in the erection of the substituted buildings within the Free State. The area in which these buildings will be constructed is left to the discretion of the Circuit Judge.'

So, the family had to return to Kerry one more time, but only to secure permission to spend the award on work elsewhere. Conveniently, Wynne Talbot-Crosbie was manager of the Scotstoun Estate Building Company, a business then erecting houses on the land of a former private estate on the outskirts of Glasgow. He now proposed to build similar properties in two Dublin suburbs, thereby satisfying the terms of the reconstruction clause. Ardfert's loss would be the capital's gain, with seventeen houses built in Glenageary and three in Howth, all designed by the same architectural practice of Higginbotham & Stafford and all very similar in appearance, of three bays, one of these being gabled, a semi-enclosed porch and red tiled roofs. Once finished, at a cost of between £1100 and £1200, the buildings were put on the market, allowing the Talbot-Crosbies to recoup the total award, and likely more besides.

And so it came to pass that the destruction of one seventeenth-century house in Kerry led to the construction of twenty suburban homes in the capital. Ardfert's loss was not just material. Left a gutted shell, the house, a rare example of late-seventeenth-century Baroque architecture in Ireland, was subsequently demolished, so that today not a trace of it survives. Ardfert Abbey's panelled hall, the walls lined with classical figures in grisaille, along with the elaborately carved staircase beyond and the building's other rooms, each bearing testament to Irish craftsmanship: all was lost along with the memories of those who had once lived here. The loss of Ardfert Abbey was more than just the disappearance of a house: with its demolition went part of County Kerry's history, never to be recovered.

4

'Considerable hostility was shown to the applicant and his servants'
DERRYQUIN, COUNTY KERRY

IN 2014, THREE YEARS before his death, Sir Christopher Bland published a novel. As he cheerfully admitted, for most of his life Bland – former chairman of the BBC, of British Telecom and the Royal Shakespeare Company – had been 'a cocktail party novelist' forever telling other people about a great idea he had for a book. Eventually he wrote *Ashes in the Wind*, an epic spanning three generations and much of the twentieth century.

Much of the novel's plot is either set in, or concerns, County Kerry, and a great house and estate there called Derriquin. The author didn't have to invent the name, since Derriquin, or Derryquin as it is more often spelled, had for hundreds of years been owned by his own forebears. Many other elements of the narrative were likewise borrowed from Bland's family background; for readers familiar with that history, the novel becomes only nominally fiction. But there is one crucial difference. In *Ashes in the Wind*, when burnt by the IRA Derriquin is still occupied by the original owners. In fact, the estate had been sold by Christopher Bland's somewhat profligate great-grandfather in 1891.

Like many other gentry families, the Blands – not least Sir Christopher – took pride in their distinguished pedigree. How gratifying for them all, therefore, that in 1826 the antiquary and librarian Nicholas Carlisle published *Collections for a History of the Ancient Family of Bland*, a work running to more than 300 pages of dense research and elevated prose. From this we learn that the Blands were of ancient Yorkshire stock, and that the first of their number to come to Ireland was an Anglican clergyman, the Rev. James Bland. Five years after taking his degree, and holy orders, at St John's College Cambridge, in 1692 he landed in Dublin as chaplain to the newly appointed Lord Lieutenant, Henry, Viscount Sydney. Chaplain might not seem a particularly distinguished office, but as many clerics discovered, daily access to the British government's representative in Ireland, at a time when all key church appointments emanated from this source, could be advantageous. In due course, the Reverend Bland became Vicar of Killarney, then Archdeacon of Aghadoe and finally Dean of Ardfert, the latter two offices being, as Nicholas Carlisle noted, 'in the Presentation of the Crown'.

All these positions were in Kerry, perhaps because the Reverend Bland had married Lucy Brewster, whose father Sir Francis Brewster, a wealthy alderman and former Lord Mayor of Dublin, had accumulated large holdings of land in the county: in 1717 Bland sold his property in Yorkshire, thereby committing himself to Ireland. Sixteen years later, by which time the Brewster property in Kerry had passed into his hands, their annual rent roll amounted to a comfortable £672.

While James and Lucy Bland's younger son, Francis, followed his father's example and became a clergyman, the elder, Nathaniel, practised law and was appointed Judge of the Prerogative Court of Dublin. Although based in Killarney, he is the first of the Blands linked to Derryquin, where, emulating his maternal grandfather, he acquired a generous tract of land and entertained ambitious plans for its improvement. Some fourteen miles west of Kenmare, the estate lay in a part of the country then scarcely developed. As late as 1837 Samuel Lewis could describe the greater part of the land here as consisting of 'rocky mountain pasture, waste, and bog, there being but a very small portion in tillage, and that chiefly for potatoes, for which sea manure is used'. Despite these limitations, in *The Ancient and Present State of the County of Kerry* (1756) topographer Charles Smith noted that

> N.Bland has built a summer lodge, with a design of reclaiming a vast adjoining bog, through which he has caused several large drains to be cut, and manured it with sea sand. Besides cutting drains, these deep stubborn morasses require to be covered with a considerable quantity of coarse gravel, in order to destroy the rank, sedgy grass, and render them sufficiently firm for cattle to graze upon; by this method a better and finer sort of grass is often produced.

Two years later in August 1758, inveterate traveller Richard Pococke, then Bishop of Ossory, ventured this far west. But then Pococke had, after all, journeyed as far as Egypt and Palestine some twenty years before, so the wilds of Kerry held little fear for him. In the journal he kept while exploring this part of the world he observed: 'We came about two leagues into Sneem harbour which is form'd by some small Island, & we went by mistake up to the north west part of the bay, into which two rivlets fall; between which Dr Bland did formerly live …'

This last observation indicates that by this date Nathaniel Bland was dead. He had married twice, a child from his first marriage displaying evidence of a certain unconventionality intermittently manifest in the family. Although called to the Bar, young John Bland fell in with a theatre troupe and decided to become an actor. According to Carlisle, the aspiring thespian was 'hissed off, by the merited indignation of his father's friends'. But perhaps the truth is that he was simply not a very good actor. Nevertheless, his love of drama remained and he became manager of the Theatre Royal in Edinburgh. He also wrote a novel, *Frederick, the Forsaken*, which, it would appear, failed to make his fortune since he died in poverty, a state exacerbated after he was disinherited by his disapproving parent.

Ironically, Nathaniel faced almost identical problems with a son of his second marriage. Like his older half-brother, Francis Bland decided he was destined to become an actor. When barely twenty and a student at Trinity College Dublin he met a young actress, Grace Phillips, thought to have been the daughter of a Welsh clergyman. The couple never married but had six children, one of them being Dorothea Bland who would likewise go on stage where she became celebrated as Mrs Jordan, one of the finest actresses of her generation. Mrs Jordan also became the mistress first of Sir Richard Ford, with whom she had three children, and then of the Duke of Clarence (future King William IV), with whom she had a further ten children. Long before then, feckless Francis Bland had abandoned Dorothea's mother, married another woman and returned to live in Kerry.

Thankfully, Nathaniel Bland's heir proved more conventional. Christened James, he followed the example of his grandfather and entered the church. According to Nicholas Carlisle, he 'had a highly cultivated mind, and was a Scholar, remarkable for the elegance and purity of his taste'. He also, it seems, wrote poems, 'none of which were published'. Their quality must therefore be imagined, which may be a blessing.

The Rev. James Bland is described as having 'succeeded to the estate of Derryquin Castle' suggesting that before the end of the eighteenth century, the family had forsaken Killarney to settle on their property in this part of the country. The same observation also indicates that by this time a house – as opposed to lodge – had been erected at Derryquin, now the centre of an estate that ran to more than 25,000 acres. Alas, the Rev. James Bland appears to have had no more luck with his children than his grandfather. Two elder sons, Nathaniel and John, were disinherited, the first for reasons unclear, the second for having married a Roman Catholic, supposedly a servant in the household of Lord Kenmare in Killarney. Thankfully, the Rev. James's third son, Francis Christopher Bland, married the respectable – and Protestant – Lucy Herbert, whose family owned extensive estates elsewhere in the county. Together the couple made sure to secure the Bland succession by having fifteen children.

Francis Christopher Bland had assisted Carlisle with his research and the indebted author duly informed readers:

> It has been the high and patriotic PRINCIPLE with this Gentleman – as it equally was with his good and conscientious Father – a PRINCIPLE which cannot be sufficiently commended or too widely circulated, TO SPEND THEIR INCOME IN THE PLACE, WHERE IT WAS PRODUCED, – And, let the '*absentees*' blush for their conduct when it is known, – that, at an early period of life, he renounced an aspiring, and often a lucrative Profession, to settle upon his '*Natale Solum*,' determined there to remain, and to contribute to the utmost of his power in the improvement of a barren soil, and the civilization of a semi-barbarous, – though, sad to relate, – an ungrateful Population!

Not everyone held Francis Christopher Bland and his estate management in such high regard. As noted, in 1837 Samuel Lewis wrote that the greater part of the property consisted of rocky mountain and bog, with very little tillage and that used chiefly for cultivating potatoes. Furthermore, 'there is at present but one main line of road through the parish; but a new line is about to be constructed from Sneem to the pass of Cameduff'.

Francis Christopher's heir, James Franklin Bland, appears to have concurred with Lewis's assessment, describing the Derryquin estate as 'a complete prairie'. After coming into his inheritance and discovering untenanted farms and lands judged to be 'completely waste' that were together losing him some £700 in annual revenue, he embarked on an extensive programme of improvements. 'Except two unfinished Board of Works roads and the main roads to Caherciveen,' he would later write, there was not a road on it. There was not a bridge over any of the four rivers which intersect the estate and which were impassable in floods, and there was not a school on the whole property. There was not a tenant who had a cart, for they had no use for them; and the whole import and export trade was done by three carriers, who went to Cork once a month or thereabouts. I have made 25 miles of roads, and can now drive to every single farm, and most of the tenants have carts and horses. I have got three schools built, to which I have contributed one-third of the cost, and have either made at my own expense, or contributed to, bridges over all the rivers.

The landlord could claim personal responsibility for at least some of the improvements on the estate, his nephew James Franklin Fuller recalling in a memoir *Omniana* (1916) that at Derryquin:

> There was a paint, oil, and glass store, the key of which my uncle (after whom, by-the-bye, I was christened James Franklin) always kept in his pocket, to guard against surprise visits from young marauders. He did the painting and glazing himself for the tenantry. This uncle was a first-rate mechanic, as well as a painter and glazier, and could do wonderful things with the lathe also.

Clearly James Franklin Bland was a man of initiative and energy, one of his friends describing him as 'An uncommonly jovial hospitable fellow, indeed he was too noisy sometimes and especially for his wife, for she was a quiet, sedate person.'

The quiet, sedate person was Emma Taylor, whose family lived nearby at Dunkerron Castle. With her husband she had four children, the eldest son being another Francis Christopher, the last of the family to live at Derryquin. While still an undergraduate at Trinity College Dublin, Francis Christopher had married Jane Hamilton, daughter of a Cork-based clergyman. The couple duly settled in Kerry where, according to a later report, he devoted himself in part to the management of the estate he duly inherited on the death of his father in 1863, and in part

> to the amusements and hospitalities of an Irish country gentleman in a county as noted then for its social pleasures as it is famous at all times for its extraordinary natural beauties. A man of commanding presence and charming address, Mr. Bland was a special favourite with his fellows, and among the tenantry his word was law. Throughout the estate, indeed, his rule was a 'benevolent despotism'.

Indeed, for some time after taking responsibility for Derryquin, Francis Christopher appears to have been as hard-working, and as popular, as his father before him. In *Disturbed Ireland: Being the Letters Written During the Winter of 1880–81* (1881), Bernard H. Becker ('Special Commissioner of the *Daily News*') wrote glowingly of the Derryquin estate's owner, informing readers:

> During thirty years he has laid out £7,000 of his own and £10,000 of Government money in bringing his estate and people somewhat into consonance with modern ideas. He has made twenty-three miles of road, built thirty stone houses with slated or tiled roofs, and three schools. When the estate came into his hands there was not a cart upon it except at Derryquin itself. Now two-thirds of the tenants have carts and horses ... The Derryquin houses or cottages are very well built and excellently planned; they are also very pretty with their whitewashed walls, red tile roofs, and doors painted red to match. These patches of bright colour give extraordinary cheerfulness to a landscape otherwise of green, brown, and grey, looking cold enough under a weeping sky.

Of course, by 1881 Francis Christopher had been in charge of the estate for less than twenty years, and not the thirty claimed by Becker, so perhaps the latter's other assertions were similarly overstated, but there is no doubt that unlike many other men in similar positions, he was popular in his area and judged a good landlord. There might have been little else said or written about the noble Mr Bland but for his having accepted an invitation in 1861 to a gathering at nearby Dromore Castle, home of an old family friend, Richard John Mahony. Earlier that year Mahony had become an evangelical Christian and he now asked the Blands to join him one evening when Charles Henry Mackintosh, preacher and ardent advocate of the Plymouth Brethren, came to speak. Mackintosh's impact was immediate and lasting: the Blands thereafter remained fervent members of the Brethren (which movement, despite a name indicating Devon origins, had in fact been founded in Dublin in the 1820s). As an obituary of Francis Christopher Bland remarked, 'Boon companions and bosom friends in recreations of their boyhood, and in the pleasures and pursuits of their early manhood, Bland and Mahony now became united in preaching Christ to their friends and neighbours.' The rest of Francis Christopher's life was devoted to preaching and prayer, and he was a renowned speaker at Dublin's Merrion Hall, which opened in 1863 and was supposedly the world's largest Brethren place of assembly (gutted by fire in 1991 so that only the façade remains, the site is now occupied by the Davenport Hotel).

Intent on spreading the Gospel word, Derryquin's owner had little time for his Kerry estate and spent less and less time there. Not that he was unfavourably regarded in the area. After all, Bernard H. Becker had described Francis Christopher Bland as 'one of the most popular men in Kerry' who had been a model landlord.

However, more preoccupied with securing his place in the next life than in the present one, Francis Christopher rather neglected the family estate. Around the mid-1860s he leased a parcel of land a short distance from the main house to academic and Church of Ireland clergyman Charles Graves (grandfather of the writer Robert Graves), then Dean of Clonfert but soon appointed Bishop of Limerick, a position he held until his death in 1899. There was a residence on this site called Parknasilla, which may have been a dower house for Derryquin; it now became the bishop's summer house. In 1891 Graves bought out the lease on Parknasilla, along with more than a hundred acres around the building. A few years later he sold the property to the Great Southern and Western Railway company, which first added bedrooms to the existing property and then built a new hotel in close proximity to it that remains in business.

At the same time as Bishop Graves bought Parknasilla, the rest of the estate was sold. Francis Christopher Bland had so failed to care for the place that it had fallen into debt. In June 1891 the *Irish Times* carried a large advertisement placed by the Chancery Division – Land Judges of the High Court announcing the imminent sale of the lands at Derryquin. In due course they were sold for £30,500. According to an obituary published after his death in London in 1894, Francis Christopher Bland, 'having obtained in heaven a better possession and an enduring one, took contentedly and even joyfully the spoiling of his earthly inheritance and left his lovely Derryquin never to return'. (Hebrews 10:34 quoted in his obituary.)

The estate's new owners were a Scottish widow and her two adult sons. Agnes Warden came from Edinburgh, as had her husband William, although he had died in 1855, the same year her youngest child, Charles Warren Warden, was born. The source of the family's wealth is unclear, although it has been proposed an earlier generation had profited from government contracts during the Napoleonic Wars at the start of the nineteenth century. After living in London, the Wardens moved to Ireland in 1882 and rented another property in County Kerry, Sheen Falls Lodge, then owned by the Marquess of Lansdowne. Ten years later, they bought Derryquin.

Not much is known about the house prior to the Wardens' acquisition. The building's design is often attributed to architect James Franklin Fuller, who had a direct link with the place; his mother Frances was a daughter of Francis Christopher Bland. In his shamelessly self-glorifying *Omniana: The Autobiography of an Irish Octogenarian* (1916), Fuller frequently refers to Derryquin. He had been born in what was usually the land agent's residence on the estate and spent much of his childhood there. However, when writing about the numerous country houses he had designed, Fuller, not a man who could ever be accused of reticence, never mentions Derryquin, even though he gives a full list of buildings in his native Kerry for which he was responsible. His involvement therefore seems unlikely.

As shown in photographs – one of which Fuller did include in his autobiography – Derryquin was a romantic, asymmetrical castle perched on an outcrop of rock by the water's edge of Kenmare Bay. Following its purchase by the Wardens, the building was thoroughly refurbished. According to Charles Warren Warden, when his family took possession of Derryquin, it was 'a comparatively small house and in bad repair'. Some might cavil at the use of the term 'small' for a property with five reception rooms, eleven bedrooms and 'a Turkish bath'. Nevertheless, over the next decade, 'the entire interior of Derryquin Castle was reconstructed, all floors, ceilings and staircases were replaced'. As well as this,

> sometimes up to sixty men were employed on the property, the average number being forty including carpenters, masons and labourers. By 1902 the reconstruction work on the old Castle was mainly finished and in that period between £20,000 and £30,000 was expended on the work, much the same sum as had been paid for its purchase. The work included an entire reconditioning of the interior of the building. The new reception rooms were either in oak or teak, the bedrooms in pitch pine with doors in either oak or teak, the windows were in teak or iron frames.

All the main reception rooms were panelled in oak, as were the outer and inner hall staircases and the first-floor landing.

During this initial period of ownership and refurbishment, Charles Warren Warden was not much involved. After attending Harrow School, he had joined the 57ᵗʰ (later Middlesex) Regiment in 1874 and saw action in the Anglo-Zulu War of 1879 where he carried the colours at the Battle of Gingindlovu and was one of the participants at the subsequent relief of Fort Eshowe. Rising to become a colonel of the Middlesex, he retired on a pension in 1895. Meanwhile, back in Ireland his mother Agnes and more importantly his older brother William were in charge.

Unlike their predecessors the Blands, the Wardens were not popular in the area. In his application for compensation following the burning of Derryquin in 1922, Charles Warden noted that even prior to the outbreak of violence during the War of Independence, he and his family had encountered 'considerable hostility'. There were ample reasons why this should have been the case, the Wardens quickly conforming to every cliché of the villainous landlord. Rents were raised, evictions became widespread, the welfare of tenants was ignored. By March 1897 questions were being asked in the House of Commons about what was taking place on the Derryquin estate, where evictions were reported to be commonplace. The Wardens insisted the last time they had undertaken such action had been almost two years earlier, the reason being that the tenant in question owed six years' rent. Furthermore, they explained, any other Derryquin tenant experiencing eviction was likewise many years in arrears. Despite pleas, the government argued it could not interfere in the management of an estate. In addition, it was claimed, the Wardens had been excellent landlords, anxious for the welfare of tenants who were being provided with help out of their difficulties, these being 'in considerable measure, due to the lax administration of the estate by its previous owners'. In other words, it was all the Blands' fault.

However, the outcry failed to die down. A year later in March 1898, the Derryquin estate was again mentioned in Westminster where it was stated the landlords had evicted a man named Sullivan after he had given shelter to an evicted tenant called Mr Neill. On the contrary, the Wardens clarified, Sullivan had long known that he would have to move out of the house he was occupying, owing to 'the filthy and insanitary state of the habitation which was in the middle of the village, and the fact that he sub-let half of it to a man with a wife and eight children. These people, with Sullivan and his son, made up the number of 12, all crowded into one small hut, with half the roof removed.'

The following month, April 1898, the socialist (and future participant in the 1916 Easter Rising) James Connolly had travelled through Kerry, and afterwards offered an alternative view of matters on the Derryquin estate. 'Six years ago,' he wrote,

> the landlord, a Scotsman, bought these lands for the sum of £32,000; the soil is very poor, composed mostly of bog and rocks, the revenue is valued by the government at £1,862, but the landlord succeeds in extorting annually £3,000 in farm rent from the unfortunate tenants, who number five hundred and thirty, and who pay rents ranging from two to four pounds sterling. This landlord exercises his rights with extreme hardness; not a stone, not a piece of wood can be taken without payment. I was told of a case where he made a farmer pay two pence for some dead branches that he had gathered on the road.

No matter how much obloquy its owners attracted, at Derryquin nothing much changed. In May 1903, for example, the nationalist MP for South Kerry John Boland spoke in Parliament of tenants still being evicted on the Warden estate, much of which was then being prepared for sale under the terms of the recently passed Land Purchase Act. By this time Colonel Charles Warden was sole proprietor. In early January 1903 his mother Agnes had died aged eighty-two, followed at the end of the following month by his brother William (aged fifty-nine). The colonel was able to benefit from the terms of the new act, although he was scrupulous about only offering tenants the worst parts of the Derryquin estate to buy, and even so insisting on being paid a premium for so-called 'Landlord's Improvements' (typically rotten fencing and post). By 1906 he had made more than £38,000 from such sales, and still retained the best parts of the property. No wonder that the previous year, in July 1905, John Boland had enquired in the House of Commons why it was necessary for Colonel Charles Warden to be given police protection, an indication of his widespread unpopularity in the area.

Eventually the colonel was left with some 5000 acres that included the village of Sneem and around 500 acres of demesne around Derryquin. Flush with cash, he now embarked on extending his home, having, as noted, dismissed the original building as a 'comparatively small house and in bad repair'. All of these drawbacks were put right with new wings added to the south and west, the former mostly given over to additional bedrooms, while the latter contained, among other spaces, a laundry, dairy and two garages. By the time the work was finished, the castle had grown to accommodate twenty-one bedrooms and dressing rooms. Derryquin's outbuildings were similarly improved and increased, with the addition, among others, of a yacht house, three barns and a carpenter's shop, new stables, a coal house and an engineer's house and even a refrigeration plant. All this cost a further £21,000 and was completed by 1911 when the colonel, by then in his mid-fifties, finally married. Aged forty, his wife Agnes was a doctor's daughter from Cambridgeshire and seems to have been either her husband's second cousin or his first cousin once removed.

Three years after the marriage and following the entry of Britain into the First World War at the start of August 1914, Colonel Warden, although by then almost sixty, volunteered for service. In the event, and no doubt due to his age – and lack of knowledge of modern warfare – he was not sent to the front but kept in England to become what were known as 'dug-outs': retired officers used to train new recruits in various regiments. He served in this capacity with a number of them before being transferred in 1917 to the recently formed Royal Defence Corps, composed of soldiers deemed too old or medically unsuited for active service.

Following the declaration of peace in November 1918, the colonel returned to Derryquin, no doubt looking forward to a comfortable old age in his smartly finished house, well attended by a wife and servants. Trouble began, he would later report, in mid-July 1921 and continued thereafter (the colonel meticulously compiled a chronology of some hundred disturbances). Initially, as so often, the incidents were relatively minor: a cottage on the estate was broken into and damaged, fruit and vegetables taken from the walled garden at night, various items stolen from outhouses. Gradually, since there were no repercussions, the intruders grew bolder. Livestock started to disappear, along with gates and fences, more and more goods removed from places like the boathouse, and timber cut down: within a year the colonel estimated he had lost £1643-worth of trees including almost 2000 firs, 125 oak, 84 elm and 615 larch.

The first raid on the main house occurred on 18 February 1922. A group of armed men turned up and demanded admittance and although some of them succeeded in getting into the entrance hall, they were pushed back out, venting their frustration by firing shots through the front door. Shrubs and other plants began to be pulled up and thrown about on the drive and in the garden, while more items from around the estate were taken almost nightly. At the start of April 1922 one of the garage doors was forced open and a motor lorry driven away. Early the following month, the colonel's own car, a Citroen, was stolen after the other garage door was broken down. Within a fortnight the motor lorry, which had been recovered, was taken again. It would be retrieved once again, only to be stolen for the third time at the beginning of July, along with another vehicle. Meanwhile, cattle were being driven off land, trees ringed to encourage their death, and still more outbuildings broken into with the further theft of tools and equipment. Inevitably the boathouse was also raided and the boats inside taken. Late one night in mid-July rocks were thrown at the castle's windows, smashing the glass and leaving the Wardens aware of their vulnerability. At the end of the month Colonel Warden reported, 'At 7p.m. armed Republicans came and viewed castle with a view to taking it over. One hit the butler in the eye with his fist.' More damage to the buildings around the estate occurred over the following days and on the morning of 9 August Askive Cottage, a substantial secondary house on the property, was set on fire; although the building was damaged, heavy rain and a lack of wind meant the flames could be quenched before it had been gutted.

Derryquin Castle and its occupants were increasingly vulnerable. By mid-August even young boys had no fear of coming onto the property, stealing fruit from the garden and breaking windows in the outbuildings. On 14 August a group of men forced their way into the house, smashing through the front door and breaking those of the main rooms on the ground floor before taking more tools and equipment from the sheds and offices. Raids on the estate were now a daily occurrence, with more items stolen and random damage done to plants, trees, gates, fences and anything else vulnerable. None of the remaining staff dared intervene: when the gardener tried to stop one group of raiders, 'They told him to mind his own business and that they would bomb him and the engineer out of the place if they were not gone in 24 hours.' Towards the end of the month, Askive Cottage was again set alight and badly damaged.

Following another raid on the castle on the night of 28 August, the Wardens left Derryquin, hoping to get help in Kenmare. The couple 'arrived here one evening at six o'clock', wrote a witness to their appearance in the town, 'just with a handbag and the clothes they stood in, having had to fly. Their servants managed to save some of the silver and a few more clothes.' The colonel appealed for assistance from members of the Free State army. The commanding officer told him no men could be spared but that he would ask headquarters for additional soldiers. For their own safety, he forbade the Wardens to return to Derryquin. Two days later, on 30 August, the castle was set alight and left a shell.

The colonel and his wife remained stranded in Kenmare for a couple of weeks before travelling to Cork in a cargo boat with a number of other passengers facing similar difficulties. They stayed two more days in Ireland and then took another boat to England. Neither of them ever returned to Derryquin, but it cannot be claimed their departure from the area was ever mourned. Eighteen months later Agnes Warden died at the age of fifty-one. The cause of her death was exophthalmic goiter, better known as Graves' Disease; the colonel was convinced the condition had been induced by stress suffered during 1921–2.

In 1925 the colonel turned seventy, but still had plenty of spirit left in him. It was needed as by then he had still not received compensation for the loss of his property in Kerry, despite producing a 95-page, leather-bound volume recording in scrupulous detail what had occurred on his estate, and what it would cost to return house and grounds to their previous state. The initial claim came to £123,920, four shillings and threepence. But there were many supplementary figures in this sum, such as lost clothing (£394 and twelve shillings) and 'sporting kit' (£78 and ten shillings). Then the colonel sought £1000 for what was described as 'loss, annoyance and general injuries (apart from any decrees obtained) caused by 100 raids by armed men' and £500 reimbursement for having to find and move into a new house, for which some furniture had to be bought.

The eventual sum sought was £92,000. When the case came up at the Quarter Sessions in Killarney, the colonel's lawyers applied for their client to give evidence in absentia, explaining he was convinced his life would be in danger should he return to Ireland to give evidence. However, after a police superintendent shared with the court his belief that Colonel Warden would be in no danger, the application was refused. In May 1928 another court sitting in Listowel awarded £42,000. This was then appealed by the County Council and eventually the colonel was granted £25,000 for the castle, £1115 for the electric light plant and £653 for the refrigeration house and plant. However, the following January, the Minister for Finance in turn appealed the court's decision, arguing the judge had erred in allowing separate amounts for the light and refrigeration plants and buildings since these were part of the main structure. The appeal was successful, the colonel's award now being capped at £25,000.

As was so often the case with these claims, even the awarded sum came with a condition attached, namely that compensation would only be paid if the old building were reinstated in whole or in part, either on the site or on one accepted by the court. Conveniently, a solution was eventually found. During this period, Dublin Corporation had embarked on constructing the country's first local authority housing estate at Marino, on the outskirts of north Dublin. Short of funds, the corporation was struggling to realize its ambitious programme when Colonel Warden's lawyers approached with a proposal: their client was prepared to sell to the council the award granted for the reconstruction of Derryquin, and at a discount. In due course, a Circuit Court Judge in Tralee allowed the 'partial reinstatement' of the colonel's old property to take place in Dublin, providing a minimum of 26 houses were built on either Griffith Avenue or as part of the Marino and Croydon Park development. The final amount received by Colonel Warden was £18,968 and ten shillings, a discount of almost a quarter on what he had been awarded and around a fifth of his original claim.

By this time he was living in Devon, having moved to the village of Buckland-Tout-Saints where in 1923, not long before the death of his wife Agnes, he bought the manor house. Restless, the colonel took to travelling on cruises, and while on one of these he met a widow from New Orleans, Anice Jones. The couple married in 1931; he was then aged seventy-five, his bride forty-seven. He finally died in 1953, aged ninety-eight and the longest-living survivor of the first Boer War. His widow had a life tenancy of the manor at Buckland-Tout-Saints: in the late 1950s it became an hotel but at the time of writing was on the market.

And what of Derryquin? After standing abandoned for some years, the shell of the old house and surrounding demesne were bought by the owners of the hotel at Parknasilla. They laid out the site as a golf course which, of course, meant people were frequently in close proximity to the ruins. This in turn led to safety concerns and so, one morning in 1969, a controlled explosion removed what had survived from the 1922 attack. A car park now occupies the ground where the house once stood and all that remains to be seen is a chimney stack arising amid bushes, and parts of the former walled garden.

5

'I do not know why I should be persecuted'
KILBOY, COUNTY TIPPERARY

ACCORDING TO AN edition of *Burke's Peerage* published in 1848, 'Henry Prittie, Esq., sustained a siege of twenty-one days in his castle of Dunalley, against the disbanded soldiers of the royal army (James II); when the besiegers at length entering, Mr Prittie was flung headlong from the top of the castle but miraculously escaped unhurt.' Did Captain Prittie, to give him his correct military title, really escape entirely unhurt? This incident must have taken place some date soon after the Battle of the Boyne (1 July 1690) and barely six months later, in January 1691, he was dead. Medicine three centuries ago was a far less exact science than is now the case but it seems reasonable to infer that the first incident might at least in part have been responsible for the second.

Captain Prittie was the son of another soldier, also called Henry, as indeed has been the case with every successive generation of the same family. Henry I appears to have been an adventuring soldier who in July 1648, while serving as a captain in the Parliamentarian New Model Army's Kentish Regiment of Horse, had defeated a superior Royalist force at Kingston. Perhaps as a result, he was a member of the Cromwellian army that arrived in Ireland the following year and was given the rank of colonel. Stationed in Carlow, in 1650 he served as High Sheriff and two years later was appointed the town's governor.

Like so many of his fellow soldiers, Colonel Prittie accepted payment for his services not in cash but land, in this instance formerly held by a branch of the O'Kennedy family and based around a castle called Dunalley in County Tipperary. Much like a number of other settlers, the colonel then increased the size of his holding by buying up parcels of land granted to other ex-soldiers, many of whom did not want to remain in Ireland and were therefore happy to dispose of their acreage, often for modest sums. For those prepared to stay and invest in their property, substantial quantities of land could be acquired and improved at reasonable cost (in 1883 Prittie's descendant the third Baron Dunalley was listed in *The Great Landowners of Great Britain and Ireland* as owning more than 21,000 acres in County Tipperary valued at £7162). In 1666, six years after the Restoration of the monarchy, Colonel Prittie was confirmed in the ownership of property running to 3642 acres in the baronies of Upper Ormond, and Owney and Arra.

Following the colonel's death in 1671, the estate he had built up was next inherited by his son, the second Henry, who seems to have lived there peaceably until his ejection from the top of the building by disgruntled Royalist troops. His son, the third Henry, then aged just eight, duly inherited the property secured by his grandfather. Despite his youth, and the death of his mother when he was still in his teens, Henry III seems to have prospered in the post-Williamite War era, and when the time came for him to marry in 1702, he established a pattern for subsequent generations by choosing an heiress for his wife: Elizabeth Harrison, only child of Colonel James Harrison of Cloughjordan. In a will made six years before his death in 1727, Colonel Harrison thoughtfully provided £100 for his 'dearly beloved son-in-law ... to buy mourning for himself and his children'. Other than serving as High Sheriff of County Tipperary, the third Henry seems to have left little impression on the country, but perhaps the hurly-burly experienced by his father and grandfather taught him the wisdom of staying quiet and staying put. His heir, Henry IV, inherited the estate in 1738, two years after marrying Deborah O'Neale, a daughter of the Venerable Benjamin O'Neale, Archdeacon of Leighlin. She had previously been married to Henry's cousin, John Bayly, with whom she had eight children before his death, and then went on to have another three more with her second husband. Naturally one of them was called Henry, the fifth of that name, who inherited not just the Dunalley estate but also his mother's fecundity, having seven children with his wife, Catherine Sadleir, although this figure rather palls when compared with the number of offspring produced by Catherine's sister Mary Trench, who had no fewer than twenty.

Catherine Sadleir was something of a catch, she and her sibling being joint heiresses of their father's County Tipperary estate. Like her mother-in-law, she had been married before, in her case to John Bury who died when the couple's only child, William (future first Earl of Charleville) was only two months old. Henry V, her second husband, pursued a more active public life than had his father and grandfather, sitting in the Irish House of Commons between 1767 and 1790. In 1800, as a reward for his son – then MP for County Carlow – voting in favour of the Act of Union, he was raised to the peerage as Lord Dunalley, taking his title from the name of the O'Kennedy castle the family had once occupied.

By that date, however, the Pritties had long abandoned the old castle for a new house. As is so often the case, no precise date is known for the construction of Kilboy, but the work may have been connected to Henry V's marriage, his wife's father Colonel Francis Sadleir having commissioned a smart residence for his family, Sopwell Hall, which dates from c. 1745. Prior to that date, the Sadleirs, like the Pritties, had occupied an old castle on the land they had acquired in the seventeenth century. Similarly, when married to her first husband, Catherine Sadleir lived in Shannon Grove, County Limerick, a charming house built in the early 1700s. She might therefore have encouraged Henry V to accommodate her somewhere better than the O'Kennedy castle he had inherited.

Volume V of *The Georgian Society Records* published in 1913 provides the following brief description of Kilboy:

> Large square house of stone, the front elevation being of considerable merit. Dining-room of stately proportions to right of hall, which is large, square and lofty, with a peculiar heavy plaster frieze. The grand stairs in large back hall have a single flight to lobby, whence the branch on either side as at Bishopscourt [County Kildare]. Windows have oak sashes, with mouldings of iron covered with copper.

The authors attributed the design of Kilboy to William Leeson, a relatively minor architect who is best remembered for laying out the new town of Westport, County Mayo, for John Browne, future first Earl of Altamont, in 1767. Possibly related to the Leeson Earls of Milltown, in the mid-1780s William Leeson appears to have been living just a few miles from Kilboy, which helps to explain why he would have received the commission to design a new house for the Pritties, as well as several others in the area attributed to him like Traverstown, Prior Park and Peterfield. Of these, Kilboy was by far the most impressive, having the appearance of an inflated villa. As *The Georgian Society Records* note, it had a fine front elevation, of three storeys over a raised basement, the top floor being treated as an attic above the entablature. Approached by a flight of stone steps, the three centre bays were demarcated by four giant engaged Doric columns beneath a pediment while the flanking bays concluded in equally massive coupled Doric pilasters. A surviving photograph indicates the side elevations were altogether more plain, their severity broken only by a generously proportioned Venetian window on the middle floor. A couple of photographs of the entrance hall included in *The Georgian Society Records* are the only extant evidence of the interior's appearance.

In January 1801, less than six months after receiving his peerage, Henry V died, both estate and title being inherited by his son, Henry

VI. For two years prior to the Act of Union, he had sat in the Irish House of Commons representing Carlow, but once the country's parliament was abolished, he sought a place at Westminster. Initially he hoped to become one of the Irish representative peers in the British House of Lords. However, efforts to achieve this goal were persistently stymied by his younger brother, Francis Aldborough Prittie, who for more than two decades represented County Tipperary in the House of Commons and regularly opposed government policy. Tainted by association, Henry VI found little support for his efforts to be a representative peer; the Duke of Richmond, then Lord Lieutenant of Ireland, wrote in 1811, 'Lord Dunalley certainly is in opposition though he states himself as unconnected with any party.'

His efforts to gain access to the House of Lords having proven unsuccessful, in 1819 Henry VI was obliged to settle for the lesser position of a seat in the House of Commons as MP for Okehampton in Devon (his Irish title not being recognized in England). Here he proved himself resolutely loyal to government policy and probably as a result, a quarter of a century after succeeding his father, he was at last able to realize a long-standing ambition and become an Irish representative peer. Other wishes had to remain unfulfilled, not least the existence of a direct male heir. Henry VI married twice, his first wife being a niece of the powerful John FitzGibbon, first Earl of Clare. Following her death, he married the Hon. Emily Maude, one of the first Viscount Hawarden's sixteen children. Alas, Henry VI and his two wives did not enjoy the same impressive rate of reproduction. When he died, Kilboy and the Dunalley title passed to a nephew, Henry VII, son of the younger brother who had for so long hindered chances of that representative peer's seat at Westminster. Other than having more children than his uncle, Henry VII, the third Baron Dunalley, appears to have left little mark on the world, even shunning the political activities of his father and uncle. Acting as High Sheriff of County Tipperary in 1840, and later as its Deputy Lieutenant can be deemed the height of his public achievements. He is remembered only for his title being used by a seafaring cousin to name the fishing village of Dunalley in eastern Tasmania. Married to Lady Anne Maria O'Callaghan, a daughter of the first Viscount Lismore, in 1885 Henry VII was succeeded by his son, Henry VIII, who towards the end of his life would see the family house burnt down.

Altogether more active than his father in the public realm, after education at Harrow and Cambridge Henry VIII had joined the Rifle Brigade and seen service during the Third Anglo-Ashanti War of 1873–4, reaching the rank of lieutenant. Two years later he married Mary Farmer, only daughter of Major-General Reginald Onslow Farmer; the couple would have six children. Although, like his grandfather he became an Irish representative peer in the House of Lords (in 1891), Henry VIII's life was primarily focused on Kilboy and Ireland. In 1883 he was appointed High Sheriff for Tipperary and served as the county's Lord Lieutenant from 1905 to 1922. He was a keen golfer and sailor (for many years keeping a boat on Lough Derg where he was commodore of the local yacht club) but also dutifully attended Church of Ireland synods, while his wife supported local charity fêtes. They both appeared at social events in Dublin during the season: at a ball in Dublin Castle given for the Duke and Duchess of Connaught in March 1902, Lady Dunalley, according to the *Irish Times*, 'was in black net over satin, trimmed with narrow blue velvet'. Five years later the same newspaper advised readers: 'Lord and Lady Dunalley and their daughter are starting shortly for Santa Brigida, at Monte, in the Canary Islands, for the remainder of the winter.'

Yet beneath this seemingly ordered existence there were already ripples of disturbance, associated as was so often the case at the time with land ownership. In July 1908 the *Irish Times* reported that a sale of meadow grass on the Kilboy estate had to be aborted following a confrontation between local farmers and labourers accompanied by a fife and drum band, and 'a large posse of police'. Following a stand-off, the crowd adjourned to a nearby field where the band played, and they were addressed by the local parish priest who condemned the police presence, insisting 'that if the clergy and he were allowed to act on their own discretion, the sale would have been carried out successfully'.

It was a taste of things to come, although at the time, like many others, Kilboy's owner was keen to divest himself of at least some of the land on his estate. After decades of tenant agitation across the country, the Land Purchase (Ireland) Act of 1903, otherwise known as the Wyndham Act, made the sale of their estates sufficiently attractive to landlords – not least by the government offering them an additional 12 per cent bonus on the eventual sale price – that there was a rush to take advantage of its terms. Such a rush, indeed, that within a few years the scheme had cost the government far more than expected or intended, with the result that official efforts were made in rein in payments to landlords. The 12 per cent bonus had only been guaranteed until November 1908, after which it was reduced to 3 per cent. The following July Lord Dunalley had to take the Treasury to court to have the full bonus paid to him: even though it had not yet taken place, the sale of a large part of the Kilboy lands to 220 tenants had been agreed before the rate fell. He won the case, but had to pay his own costs. Previously running to some 18,000 acres, the estate now shrunk to 2000.

When war with Germany was declared in 1914, like many others of their class, the Dunalleys' two sons immediately signed up. For the younger, the Hon. Francis Prittie, it proved a relatively brief conflict: a captain in the Rifle Brigade, he was killed in December 1914 and buried in a Belgian cemetery. The elder, future fifth Baron Dunalley, was more fortunate. Likewise enrolled in the Rifle Brigade, he had previously fought in the second Boer War at the start of the century. Although wounded, he survived the war, was mentioned in despatches, awarded the Distinguished Service Order in 1916 and retired a major.

Back in Ireland, despite their loss, his parents made their own contribution to the war effort, Lord Dunalley chairing recruitment meetings in Nenagh, his wife acting as president of a local branch of the Red Cross and of a soldiers' home, which opened in Templemore. Following the cessation of hostilities in November 1918, they might well have imagined their old way of life would resume, but this was not the case. Amid the growing popular clamour for independence, Lord Dunalley, still a representative peer in the House of Lords, became associated with the London committee of the Irish Unionist Alliance, the organization which had since the late nineteenth century been campaigning to maintain the union with Britain. Those members who lived in the southern part of the country, including Dunalley, would eventually see their hopes dashed, and in April 1921 Dunalley's name was included in an official list of peers considered eligible to be elected as members of the new Free State's Senate.

Unlike some other members of his class, he chose not to take up the position, having just turned seventy. His grandson Terence Prittie would remember him from this time as 'a towering figure, with a mane of white hair and a big, white, walrus moustache which tickled intolerably when he kissed you'. Lady Dunalley, on the other hand, 'seemed completely colourless, save that she had a character of iron and, unknown to us children, in fact dominated her proud and patriarchal husband. She was English, and inhibitingly reserved ...' Yet the couple were well liked in the area, the record of the family not being besmirched by acts of cruelty to their tenants. According to Terence Prittie, during the Great Famine, the second Lord Dunalley

> produced money to buy cheap food for the starving and to give employments by building the 'famine roads' up the mountain, which were used by the poor to go up and cut peat, to burn in their homes and warm them. There were no hideous 'rack-rents' ... the rent for a cottage could be as low as five shillings a year, and our agriculturally poor and usually waterlogged estate was to become financially unviable on such a basis.

Despite being well regarded in the locality, during the course of the War of Independence, the Dunalleys did not remain immune from attack. In July 1921 Tipperary's County Inspector reported that 'the rebels and the ill-disposed are seizing the opportunity to swoop down on houses that escaped the attention of marauders during the stormiest period'. He might have been referring to Kilboy, which the previous month had suffered the first of what were to be many robberies over the course of the year ahead, in this instance the pilfering of a number of items from garages near the house. The following November the house itself was raided with a diverse range of items stolen. Along with obviously pilferable objects, such as pieces of silver tableware (a tea pot worth £25, sugar bowl and tongs £16, six teaspoons £10 and so forth), the looters carried away brass finger bowls, a silk muffler, safety razors, a box of cigars, six pairs of stockings, a couple of overcoats and cufflinks to a total value of £250, suggesting they were guided by opportunism rather than any clear strategy.

From the beginning of 1922 raids on the estate grew steadily more frequent, and more brazen. In late February 1922, for example, a seven-year-old filly was taken, together with a number of harnesses, some motor tyres and tubes, and several cushions, the total valued at £136. Four weeks later, three pure-bred Friesian bulls (together worth £190) were stolen from the estate, with more cattle disappearing over several dates in early April, along with the gates that had hitherto kept them within their fields. During the same period, substantial stands of trees were vandalized, either cut down or so badly damaged as to make them worthless: 188 oaks in part of the estate (value £188), 88 beech and 277 Scotch fir in another (£40 and £138 respectively), and around 1000 young larch, 200 ash, 150 oak and 150 spruce in a third (£2000, £100, £150 and £300). In total, their value came to £1916, for which the estate would eventually receive £470, twelve shillings and threepence. During the same period, some 400 yards of stake and wire fencing, as well as the same amount of netting, were also stolen. More gates and doors vanished, along with further livestock.

Between late June and early July another 800 trees 'were wantonly and maliciously cut down and destroyed'.

By then, Kilboy's septuagenarian owners had quite understandably left the property, life at Kilboy having become intolerable for them. They were baffled by what was happening. 'I do not know why I should be persecuted,' Lord Dunalley exclaimed. Early in the morning on 8 May, while they were still living there, the house was again raided by a group of men. As on the previous occasion in November, an eclectic range of items was taken including a heavy great coat valued at £7, a watch and its chain (£15 and £13 respectively), six vests worth £3 in total, two pairs of fish knives and forks (£2), a bicycle (£15) and a waterproof apron (eight shillings). More frightening, there had been several attempts made on the couple's lives, the first occurring on the morning of 28 May when shots were fired at Lord Dunalley while he was on his way to church. Normally he drove his car in a highly erratic fashion but on this particular occasion he chose to take a pony and trap: following gunfire, only the pony sustained an injury. Other similar attacks soon followed; on one occasion the couple were standing on the front steps of the house when someone hidden in the shrubbery took a shot at them, the bullet lodging in a windowsill. As Terence Prittie remarked, 'Too much enthusiasm, or too much liquid refreshment, may have caused the daringly concealed marksman to miss these two unarmed and absolutely harmless old people. Apart from his eccentricities on the road, my grandfather was a steady, sensible and hard-working citizen.' Although their solicitor John Howard Dudley wrote that he had been informed by a member of the Free State army that the shot might have come from the gun belonging to a guard 'while bent on sporting in the grounds and not intended for you at all', the Dunalleys no longer felt safe and decided to move to England, leaving the estate's steward, Samuel Doupe, in charge. The latter soon experienced his own troubles, the house he occupied being broken into and the raiders shooting him in the left hand, rendering it thereafter almost useless. The house was then set on fire, destroying most of his personal possessions. Nevertheless, he stayed on, moving into Kilboy since the Dunalleys had left.

As the situation continued to deteriorate and the government appeared less and less able to bring members of the anti-Treaty forces under control, Dudley had to agree with the couple's decision to go, commenting, 'I think it was just as well you left when you did.' On 17 July he urged Lord Dunalley to order vans 'to have the furniture removed from Kilboy House and stored in Dublin for I am greatly afraid the house will be burned or destroyed. It may not be easy for them to manage it as in many places the roads are blocked but at any rate they could try and if possible the removal could be effected in one day.' Later the same week he repeated this proposal, noting that many fences around Kilboy had been pulled down and 'sections of the land actually being grazed by trespassers'.

There was another raid on the house, armed men turning up at midnight demanding to be admitted. The occupants, Doupe and other members of staff, were locked in a room after which the raiders ransacked the place, taking clothes and footwear, linen and other items, in total estimated to be worth £150. Aware that the house was vulnerable to further, possibly fatal, attack, its owner sent a telegram to his solicitor in Dublin, asking if protection for the property could be provided by the Ministry of Defence. The solicitor duly went to the ministry, then in Portobello Barracks, but was unable to see anyone about the matter, so then sent a letter seeking help:

> We do not think that Lord Dunalley would have telegraphed to us unless he had received some special information that his house was in danger, and that being so, we trust that you have been able to arrange for its protection. Of course we know that it would not be possible to send a guard to every house the owner of which was nervous and feared that it might be attacked, but where there is particular reason for supposing that a house is to be attacked we take it that the position is different. Lord Dunalley's house is of

course a large one, and a number of people are depending on his
establishment being kept up and we are sure that this will have
weight with you.

Whether it did or not, and despite further telephone calls and letters to
the ministry – all answered with the same assurances that the matter
would receive attention – no protection was provided.

The denouement came in the early hours of 3 August. Afterwards
Samuel Doupe wrote to his employer, 'My lord, Kilboy House is in
ruins and the front yard is burnt to ashes. I don't know what to do.'
As before, a group of men arrived at the building and, after being
refused entry, smashed down a door to gain access. According to his
employer, 'the night the raiders burnt my house they consulted for an
hour as to whether they should shoot him [Doupe] then and there or
not, and he was present'. Eventually Doupe and his wife, together with
the handful of other servants still living on the premises, were taken to
an outbuilding while gallons of petrol brought for the purpose were
spread around the floors before being set alight. Only when the house
was beyond salvation did the raiders leave, and although the alarm
was then raised and help arrived, it was too late. Many years later, the
sixth Lord Dunalley would jocularly suggest that the house had been
burnt down by a group of schoolchildren: 'I'm sure they had a lot of
fun. After all, it's not every day of the week that one gets the chance
to set fire to a Georgian mansion.' Given what had been happening
over previous months, the suggestion that the blaze was due to a gang
of juvenile delinquents seems not very credible.

Doupe and the others did what they could to rescue items from
the burning building. According to the sixth Lord Dunalley, 'They
threw everything they could out the windows onto the lawns, and the
farm workers continued to turn up for work through heavily armed
pickets.' His younger brother Terence Prittie would write, 'Gallantly,
they dragged out mahogany wardrobes believed to be "Her Ladyship's
favourite" and left all the decent furniture behind. The family pictures

were laboriously cut out of the frames, which were worth rather more than the pictures inside them. A few other odds and ends were saved.' Among the 'odds and ends' were two pianos, one a Broadwood in the entrance hall, and sundry pieces of furniture from the main rooms, moved into the yard beside the house. But much of this was then lost, when a further raid took place the following night and the yard set on fire. On this occasion the outer farmyard was looted and, as Doupe wrote to Lord Dunalley, all agricultural machinery and implements, in fact anything of value, carried off. 'The stables, the main conservatory and the kitchen conservatory, the kitchen and the main gardens are all looted, broken and destroyed.' Over the next few days, further raids saw both the gardener's and the yardsman's houses gutted by fire, with the storehouse and estate workshop, along with a rick of hay.

What, from the main house, was lost in the fire? Terence Prittie referred to the value of the picture frames and indeed, a list of twenty-seven of these, or at least of their dimensions, was subsequently compiled, their total value estimated to be £174. It seems most of the pictures they held were saved, but this was not the case with the books that once filled the shelves of Kilboy's library. In a list of items destroyed in that room, reference was made to 3000 books, 'many dating from 1600', without providing information on what these were. The eventual compensation claim simply noted the loss of 'Library and odd volumes about 6,000 altogether' valued in total as worth £5000. Repeated requests from the Dunalleys' solicitor for 'any sort of list or catalogue of even the more important and rarer books, and a general description as to what the library contained' failed to elicit results. On the other hand, more detail was given on the library's furnishings, such as five mahogany armchairs with fluted legs deemed to have been worth £50, an Italian inlaid maple card table £15, and three pairs of brocade curtains £25. In 1943 genealogist Thomas Sadleir, who was related to the Pritties, wrote an account of the relatively meagre family papers still remaining and briefly mentioned those lost in the fire, which he had examined when staying at Kilboy thirty-five years earlier. They included a number of letters written when young men by the future George IV and his brother Frederick, Duke of York. These, Sadleir remarked, were 'characterised by bad grammar, atrocious spelling and often unseemly language'. The letters were among the material burnt in August 1922.

So was much else besides, as laid out in an itemized report on the house contents produced at the time compensation was sought. One page of this is entirely devoted to estimating the cost of Kilboy's collection of dead animals, produced for the Dunalleys by a London taxidermy company, Rowland Ward of Piccadilly. Three African buffalo skulls and horns were worth £50, those of six waterbucks £20 and those of four Himalayan ibex £10. By far the most costly items were two ancient Irish elk skulls, together priced at £125. Little else in the house was judged as valuable as the pair of skulls, although a carved mahogany sideboard in the dining room was priced at £175 and an Axminster carpet in the drawing room was priced at £150. Also in the latter room, a carved white marble chimney piece was worth £75 and the cut-glass chandelier, fitted for electric light, £50. Back in the dining room, another old mahogany sideboard was valued at £100, as were both the Parian and Siena marble chimney piece and a mahogany wine table (although the four-segment dining table was only deemed worth half that amount). Page by page, every lost possession is itemized, down to clothes left behind by the Dunalleys, such as his peer's uniform (£40) and coronet (£10). His wife likewise lost her uniform and coronet, along with a green-and-gold brocade dress (£50) and several others of satin in different colours, each worth £25, although her most valuable item was a bearskin rug (£100).

Doupe, the Dunalleys' long-serving land steward, soon found himself targeted, and in October 1922 he was warned that his life was in danger if he did not leave the estate. By then, his spirit was crushed by the previous months' events. As far back as mid-August, he had written to his employer, 'the people are gone mad here, it breaks my heart to see the place now, I hardly know what I am doing'. Finally in November he moved to Ulster, finding employment on the Blessingbourne estate in County Tyrone, albeit on a lower salary than he had earned at Kilboy. In 1926 he applied to the Irish Grants Committee for compensation, describing himself as 'physically a broken man' and seeking £840 to make up for his losses: in August 1927 he was awarded £150.

Meanwhile, like so many other estate owners whose property had been damaged or destroyed, the Dunalleys embarked on the long process of seeking compensation for their losses. Despite what had happened, and their ages (they were both by now over seventy), the couple were determined to return to Ireland as soon as possible. Their solicitor in Nenagh was doubtful whether this was a good idea, writing in May 1923 that even if s a smaller house were built in Kilboy, its owner

> would never be able to carry on there and farm there as he did before, nor do I think it would be safe for him to attempt to do so at any rate for a good long time to come ... I think he would only be able to keep a very small portion of the land formerly in his own hands in the Demesne proper, and that all the outside portion would have to be sold, either voluntarily or by compulsion.

Undaunted, the Dunalleys lodged their claim. Initially they sought £100,000 for loss of the house and its contents, together with various outbuildings, but following more detailed valuations this was reduced to £75,508, one shilling and sixpence. They may have been encouraged in these intentions by the thought that their daughter-in-law, Beatrix Graham, married to the future fifth Lord Dunalley, had a wealthy father, James Noble Graham. He had made a fortune in large part from the importation of port wine (his name survives in the firm of Graham's Port) but then seems to have over-extended himself and in 1923, just as the Dunalleys began to think about rebuilding Kilboy, Graham was declared bankrupt. No financial assistance would therefore be forthcoming from that source.

Nor indeed, did it seem likely to come from anywhere else, although an advance of £5000 was provided by the British government in November 1923, on the understanding that it would be recovered from any subsequent award. Throughout the year, a court hearing into the family's claim for compensation was scheduled to be heard in Ireland on a number of occasions, but kept being postponed. In January 1924 Lord Dunalley wrote directly to the president appealing for his help in having the case heard: 'Of course I know the Government's difficulties to a certain extent and sympathise with them, but I think it would be for the good of all of us if the matter could be settled soon.' Finally, in May 1924, an award of £9534 was made with respect to the loss of Kilboy's contents and other goods. Two months later the question of compensation for the house came to court: £58,537 had been sought but only £17,395 granted (plus £292, nineteen shillings and threepence for expenses), and the payment of this was conditional on full reinstatement of the lost building. Some of this sum (almost £1164) was due in arrears on local rates and would therefore be paid to the county council instead.

There then followed the inevitable delays in securing the monies promised, paid out in stages as work on Kilboy's reconstruction progressed, but always late and always only after the architect responsible for the job, Brian Sheehy of Limerick, as well as the Dunalleys' solicitor, had written to the Department of Finance pointing out that the funds were now overdue. In June 1926, for example, the solicitor wrote asking when some payment could be expected because

> we must be in a position to advise Lord Dunalley as to his financial liabilities and resources, now that he has made up his mind to return and live in his old family home the rebuilding of which we are pleased to say is rapidly advancing but the demands on his financial resources are also rather a strain when he has so many liabilities to meet.

The final payment was only received at the end of January 1931.

By then work on rebuilding Kilboy was well completed, the architect having signed off on the job in February 1927. Externally, the building looked much as it had before, although without its former top storey. The main rooms were oak panelled in an eighteenth-century style, the previous bifurcating staircase replaced by a simpler one of the same wood. The family could now return to their old home, but six months later Lord Dunalley died; he was then aged seventy-six. His wife would follow him in 1929. Their surviving son, another Henry, succeeded to what remained of the estate. As his younger son Terence Prittie would later write:

> My grandparents went into exile in England, but it was their firm intention to return to the estate on which the family had lived for two and a half centuries. They returned less than five years later, only for my grandfather to die within months, leaving both house and title to my father. Unfortunately, they chose to return to a grandeur which was no more than a facade. Eventually, there was some governmental compensation for the destruction of our family home, but it was far from adequate. Yet my grandparents rebuilt virtually on the old, grand scale. The financial resources on which they drew while in England were further depleted by building and re-furnishing costs. The estate, never prosperous after much of it had been sold under various Land Acts, was doomed unless an heir to it married an heiress for the filthy lucre which was needed.

Nevertheless, he remembered it as a wonderful childhood home: 'There was a lake where one could fish or bathe. There were acres of garden and woodland in which there was much to do – old trees to be cut down, paths now choked with undergrowth to be cleared, small ponds to be cleaned out, streams to be damned in order to catch small fish to stock the lake.' Superficially, all seemed to be well, although

Terence Prittie later realized that despite appearances to the contrary, the family were living at Kilboy on borrowed time. 'My father,' he wrote, 'did not seem to worry at all; he had, in fact, given up before he even tried to manage his inheritance.' The truth emerged only when the fifth Lord Dunalley died in May 1948: the Kilboy farm had been losing at least £1000 per annum. In addition, for the previous seven years, its owner had not even bothered to take care of any financial correspondence: 'bank managers' letters lay unopened in his desk. There was a huge tax-bill outstanding on the sale of timber, and huge overdrafts in two banks.' His heir, the sixth Lord Dunalley, struggled for some years to keep going, attempting various economies such as pulling down in 1952 the vast house his grandparents had only rebuilt a quarter century earlier and in its place constructing a modest bungalow.

But it was to no avail and by the late 1950s what remained of the Kilboy estate was on the market. In 1960 it was bought by an Irish-American industrialist, Norman Butler, who lived there for some time before offering the place for sale once again in the mid-1970s. Kilboy was then bought by businessman and founder of Ryanair Tony Ryan who lived in the house until he bought another estate, Lyons in County Kildare. Following his death in 2007, Kilboy was inherited by Ryan's youngest son Shane who had already applied for planning permission to demolish the 1950s bungalow and construct a version of the original house on its raised, rusticated basement, the only part of the building to survive. Designed by Quinlan and Francis Terry, the new Kilboy is now home to Shane Ryan and his family.

Spiddal House, County Galway: the drawing room as designed in 1908 for Martin Morris by William Alphonsus Scott. Courtesy of Redmond Morris, 4th Baron Killanin.

Spiddal House, County Galway: the drawing room in the aftermath of the arson attack that gutted the building in April 1923. Courtesy of Redmond Morris, 4th Baron Killanin.

Spiddal House, County Galway: an extraordinary synthesis of Hiberno-Romanesque and Byzantine styles, the building was reconstructed in a simpler style some years after the arson attack to the design of architect Ralph Henry Byrne. Courtesy of Redmond Morris, 4th Baron Killanin.

Bingham Castle, County Mayo: an undated photograph of the castellated house built for Denis Bingham at the start of the nineteenth century. Courtesy of the Irish Architectural Archive.

Ardfert, County Kerry: a late nineteenth-century photograph showing the house with its great forecourt. Private collection.

Ardfert, County Kerry: the drawing room with its heavy plastered ceiling and walls hung with family portraits. Private collection.

Ardfert, County Kerry: the panelled entrance hall with its richly carved doorcase and walls decorated at some unknown date in the eighteenth century with near life-size grisaille figures in classical dress. Private collection.

Derryquin, County Kerry: a view of the castellated house from Kenmare Bay showing the improvements and extensions made by Colonel Charles Warren Warden. Courtesy of the Irish Architectural Archive.

Kilboy, County Tipperary: an advertisement offering the rebuilt house offered for sale by the sixth Lord Dunalley.

Cappoquin House, County Waterford: a watercolour of the house, then called Belmont, dated 1843. Courtesy of Sir Charles Keane.

Cappoquin House, County Waterford: the building left a shell in the aftermath of being burnt in February 1923. Courtesy of Sir Charles Keane.

Cappoquin House, County Waterford: a photograph taken in the stableyard and showing the work of reconstruction underway. Courtesy of Sir Charles Keane.

*Barbavilla, County Westmeath: the carved segmental pediment over the main
entrance of the house showing the arms of the Smyth family.
Courtesy of the estate of Paddy Rossmore.*

*Clonyn Castle, County Westmeath: the vast, gloomy house designed in the early 1870s
by John McCurdy for the first Lord Greville. Courtesy of the National Library of
Ireland via Flickr Commons, NLI Ref: L_CAB_03198.*

Bessborough, County Kilkenny: an early twentieth-century postcard by commercial photographers A. H. Poole of Waterford showing alterations made to the façade by the seventh Earl of Bessborough.

Desart Court, County Kilkenny: the house rebuilt after being gutted by fire, but then abandoned and unroofed, and awaiting demolition.
Courtesy of the Irish Architectural Archive.

'The beginning of our family's severance with Ireland.'
CAPPOQUIN, COUNTY WATERFORD

ON 8 JANUARY 1930, the *Irish Independent* reported that over 150 guests had attended a ball held the previous evening at Cappoquin House to mark the imminent twenty-first birthday of Richard Keane. 'Surpassing in brilliance and gaiety most entertainments of the season,' the newspaper's readers learnt, 'last night's ball was remarkable for the variety and design of the ladies' dresses.' But even more remarkable was the fact that just seven years earlier the building had been left a smouldering ruin. On 20 February 1923 Richard's father Sir John Keane, who had been visiting his wife and children in London, wrote in his diary, 'Crossed to Dublin ... on arrival learnt that Cap Ho. had been burnt, main house completely destroyed, but servants' wing and stables escaped ... This marks a stage in one's Irish life. It is sad to lose one's home where one's people have been for over 150 years + especially such a fine well decorated house.'

Otherwise known as Belmont, Cappoquin House had, as noted by Sir John, been the residence of successive generations of his forebears since it was built in the 1770s. Originally called Ó Catháin (O'Cahan) and otherwise anglicized as Kean, Cane, Cahan and Caine, the family could trace its origins back to the early Middle Ages. Nineteenth-century genealogist John O'Hart credited the O'Cahans with being descended from one Conchobhar (Connor), Prince of Leim-an-

Madaidh (Limavady) 'and a younger brother of Niall Frasach, the 162nd Monarch of Ireland'. Whatever about the accuracy of this, certainly from the twelfth century onwards the family were settled in the barony of Keenaght in what is now County Derry. The branch that came to live at Cappoquin had as their ancestor one Donall, or Daniel, O'Cahan who lived in the Keenaght area in the early 1500s. But the family's fortunes declined steeply over the course of the next century, primarily owing to their affiliation with the hitherto-dominant O'Neill clan. Following the departure from Ireland of Hugh O'Neill, Earl of Tyrone in 1607, the O'Cahans were left exposed; the last significant member, Donnell Ballach O'Cahan (who was for a time Lord Tyrone's son-in-law) spent his final years ignominiously locked in the Tower of London.

Subsequently displaced from their ancestral lands in Ulster, the family was, like so many others, banished west of the Shannon to Connacht. The memory never left them; as Sir John Keane would ask another member of the Irish Senate during a debate, 'Does he realise that in my blood there is a record of knowledge of confiscation and oppression just as great as any member of this House? My ancestors were driven out of the Ó Catháin country by the British in the Elizabethan days.'

However, following the victory of William of Orange at the Battle of the Boyne in 1690, one member of the family, George O'Cahan, more pragmatic than earlier generations, recognized that only by conforming to the rules of the new governing order could he hope to thrive. Consequently, he converted to the Established Church and entered government service as a lawyer (a profession then closed to Roman Catholics under Penal legislation). He also anglicized his surname to Keane. None of this was particularly unusual: a relative, Richard O'Cahan, likewise joined the Established Church and changed his name before joining the army to fight against James II's forces. After participating in the defence of Derry in 1689, Kane was a member of the Williamite army at both the Battle of the Boyne and the Siege of

Limerick, then participated in both the Seven Years' War and the War of the Spanish Succession. Rising to the rank of general, he ended his career as Governor of Menorca, dying in its capital Mahón in 1738 as is noted on a monument to his memory in Westminster Abbey.

George Keane's pragmatism was therefore not unusual, and indeed he and his descendants duly prospered since in July 1738 his son John was able to lease 7313 acres in County Waterford from Richard Boyle, fourth Earl of Cork and third earl of Burlington. The term was for 999 years at £500 per annum. On this land had once stood an old FitzGerald castle, replaced in the sixteenth century by an Elizabethan mansion built after the territory had been granted by Elizabeth I in 1589 to one of her favourites, Sir Christopher Hatton. It occupied the site of what is now Cappoquin House, situated at a strategic point on the Blackwater: having meandered eastwards, the river now turns ninety degrees before heading south to enter the sea by the port of Youghal, County Cork, some twenty miles away. The ground rises steeply above the fast-moving water, offering views for many miles around and making it the ideal location both for a defensive castle and, in due course, a classical house.

John Keane died in 1756 and, it appears, his heir Richard followed him to the grave soon afterwards, since the Waterford lands were then inherited by the next generation, another John, presumably a minor at the time having only been born in 1757. As soon as he reached the age of twenty-one and could take charge of his own affairs, he married a local woman, Sarah Kelly, whose family lived just a few miles away in Lismore. The couple would have three sons before Sarah's death, after which John Keane, by then a baronet, married again in 1804, his second wife, Dorothy Scott, being a similarly widowed Englishwoman with whom he had one more son. As befitted a country gentleman at the time, he stood for parliament, representing Bangor from 1790–7 in the Irish House of Commons, and then Youghal in the years immediately preceding the abolition of the Irish parliament in 1800. The following year he received his baronetcy and continued to represent Youghal at Westminster until 1806. George O'Cahan's decision just over a century earlier to change his surname and religion had proven a wise one.

It was the first Sir John Keane who is believed to have commissioned a new house at Cappoquin in the late 1770s, seemingly having bought out the original lease taken on by his grandfather. The property's architect remains unknown although John Roberts (1712–1796), responsible for many other notable buildings in Waterford city and County, has often been proposed. A claim has also been made for Davis Ducart, an architect and engineer whose origins are unclear (he may have been born in northern Italy) and whose list of attributable works is in almost constant flux. Stylistically, the house could have come from the hand of either man, or just as easily from that of someone else. An unsigned note among the family's papers states that Italian craftsmen were employed here between 1775 and 1780, but this may be just fanciful conjecture; speaking at the launch of the original Irish Georgian Society in February 1908, the organization's president, Professor John Pentland Mahaffy, had decried 'the vulgar belief that all the good work in Dublin was done by Italians, whilst our people were looking on helplessly'. Suggesting your house had been designed by an Italian was for long thought to give the building a certain cachet. More likely craftsmen working in the Waterford area were responsible for the construction and decoration of Cappoquin House, In *Georgian Mansions in Ireland* (1915), architect Page L Dickinson, who had been employed by Sir John Keane to carry out work on the building two years earlier, reported: 'In Waterford there seems to have been a highly skilled local school, and excellent specimens of their work exist at Cappoquin House.' We shall probably never know for certain who was responsible.

Some seventy feet long and sixty-five feet deep, the building's south-facing, seven-bay facade of pale grey sandstone ashlar rises two storeys over basement, its parapet finished with a line of urns. The central three-bay breakfront has tall arched windows on both ground and first floors. The two sides of the house, each of six bays, are finished in the same manner as the facade, but the north side, which looks into the stable yard, is left in unfinished rubble stone. No early images of the house survive other than an 1843 watercolour signed 'R Armstrong'. This shows the old conservatory on the east side of the dining room. Also apparent is that the main block was not then attached to the servants' wing, which helps to explain why the latter survived the fire of February 1923. The interior appears to have followed the model typical of Irish country houses at the period, with an entrance hall off which open to the rear the drawing and dining rooms respectively. Behind a screen of columns (another very typical decorative device) lay the staircase hall, with additional rooms, including the library and morning room, before a back hall gave access to the yard. Little else is known about the internal appearance of the house. In his diary entry the day after place had been gutted by fire, Sir John Keane lamented, 'I now wish I had good interior photographs.'

This, then, is all that is known about the residence built by the first Sir John Keane and, following his death in April 1829, inherited by his eldest son Richard. By now the Keanes were thoroughly integrated into the British Establishment. Sir John had served in Parliament, and his sons would all serve in the army. True, Sir Richard's experience only extended as far as becoming a lieutenant-colonel in the local militia, but his siblings had more exacting military careers. The youngest, George Michael Keane, son of his father's second marriage, became a colonel in the 2nd Foot. Meanwhile Edward Keane took an active part in the Napoleonic Wars, serving under the future Duke of Wellington in the Peninsula. He later acted as aide-de-camp to Sir Richard Hussey Vivian, and at the Battle of Waterloo served with Henry Paget, future Marquess of Anglesey, afterwards being promoted to the rank of major (he eventually rose to become a colonel). By far the most distinguished military record was achieved by another brother, John Keane, who first entered the army in 1793, participating in a succession of campaigns so that by the time he fought at the Battle of New Orleans in January 1815 he had already been made a major-general. In the aftermath of the Napoleonic Wars, he acted as Commander-in-Chief in the West Indies and administered the colonial government of Jamaica. Then, in the 1830s, he became Commander-in-Chief of the Bombay Army, and at the end of that decade, commanded the British and Anglo-Indian armies during the first Anglo-Afghan War, the opening move in what came to be known as the Great Game: a long-running struggle between the Russian and British empires for control of this part of Central Asia. Keane's was the first of many such interventions by Western powers that, almost two centuries later, has still not reached a happy outcome. But at the time, he seemed to have ensured the upper hand for the British, winning what appeared to be a decisive victory at the Battle of Ghazni in July 1839 before going on to take Kabul. Within three years many of these gains had been lost, a British army massacred and another force, this time led by General William Nott, was back in Afghanistan. By then, Keane had long returned home and was enjoying the fruits of his victory: in its aftermath, he had been created Baron Keane, and granted an annual government pension of £2000 for himself and his next two heirs (very conveniently, the title died out following the death of the childless third Lord Keane in 1901).

Lord Keane's elder brother, Sir Richard, outlived him by eleven years before being succeeded in 1855 by his own eldest son, Sir John Keane, third baronet, who seems to have led a thoroughly unremarkable life (even *Burke's Peerage and Baronetage*, usually so diligent in finding something to praise about its subjects, can find nothing to report about Sir John other than the dates of his birth, two marriages and death). But this superficially uninteresting account conceals one exceptional achievement: he saved the family estate from sale to strangers. In 1855, when Sir John, then aged thirty-nine, inherited Cappoquin, the property came with some 11,400 acres in counties Waterford and Tipperary. This was now all placed on the open market by the Encumbered Estates Court, a body established by acts of Parliament in 1848–9, in the aftermath of the Great Famine. The purpose of the court was to facilitate the sale of Irish property, the owners of which were so indebted that they could not hope to meet their financial obligations: between 1849 and 1858, some 3000 landed estates running to five million acres were sold in this way. Not just Cappoquin, but several other estates along the River Blackwater, including Strancally and Ballysaggartmore, came on the market during this period as a result.

Many years later, the third baronet's grandson, the next Sir John Keane, would conclude that Cappoquin had almost been lost as a result of poor management, and presumably excessive expenditure, by earlier generations. In his diary for March 1897, he observed, 'This estate must have been in a great mess for many years prior to the sale in the landed estates court – the Colonel and his father Sir Richard do not appear to have done much to solve a difficulty.' The 'Colonel' in this case was presumably the second baronet's brother, Colonel Henry Keane, who may have had the job of managing the estate. In 1855, divided into twenty-two lots and reckoned by assessors to have an annual valuation of £4967 (although an independent assessor valued them at £5625), the Keane lands were due to be sold in mid-November. The first fourteen lots, running to a little more than 4000 acres, went under the hammer, but the rest – running to around 7300 acres – were bought back by Sir John Keane for £38,810. How had this been achieved? Surviving documents provide no explanation, but it appears that the necessary help was provided by Sir John's father-in-law, Richard Keatinge, Judge of the Prerogative Court of Ireland, who didn't want to see his daughter Laura and her children left without a home.

Having succeeded in avoiding the complete loss of his family property, the third baronet understandably preferred to live quietly at Cappoquin, unnoticed by anyone, even the authors of *Burke's*. When he died in 1881, he was able to hand the property on to the next generation, his elder son, another Richard. However, there were soon fresh challenges to be met. When Sir Richard came into his inheritance, the Keanes' land holding had increased to 8909 acres, with an annual value of £3227; despite their owning more land, the family's annual income had declined due to falling agricultural prices caused by cheaper imports from the other side of the Atlantic Ocean. Now, growing agitation among tenants for lower rents, and soon after for land ownership, began creating new difficulties for Sir Richard and other members of his class. A succession of acts passed by the British Parliament sought to appease both tenants and landlords, the first in 1870 with a second following in the same year Sir Richard's father had died and he had taken over responsibility for the estate. Pragmatically, the new baronet sent a printed letter to tenants assuring them, 'I am fully prepared to accept this land act in the spirit in which it is framed,' and advising that should he and they have any difference of opinion, the tenants could, with his approval, seek resolution from the land courts.

Sir Richard was only responsible for the Cappoquin estate for eleven years, dying at the age of forty-seven in October 1892 and leaving a wife and four children, the youngest aged eleven. His widow, Adelaide Sidney, was the elder daughter and, after her unmarried sister's early death, sole heiress of John Vance, who had served as MP for Dublin City (1852–65) and Armagh City (1867–75). An ardent unionist, Vance is credited with being the first person to equate Irish demands for self-government with excessive Roman Catholic influence; during a House of Commons debate in July 1871 he declared 'his own opinion was that "home rule" in Ireland would prove to be "Rome rule"'. The Vance family lived in 18 Rutland (now Parnell) Square, today known as the Dublin Writers Museum. In the first half of the 1890s, the building's interiors were elaborately remodelled for its next owner, George Jameson (a member of the whiskey distilling family), which perhaps explains why one of the original eighteenth-century chimney pieces should have ended up at Cappoquin House. Likely dating from the late 1760s (when the Rutland Square house was built), the chimney piece is of Carrara marble with verde antico marble inserts and carved panels and is today in the South Hall.

It was not here but in the Vance family home that the fifth Keane baronet, Sir John – hereafter referred to simply by his surname – was born in June 1873, the eldest of four children. He was just nineteen when his father died and at the time attending the Royal Field Artillery, Woolwich, from which he graduated the following year. Given their family history, it was almost inevitable that both his brothers would also serve in the British armed forces, the elder of the two, George Keane, becoming a captain in the Royal Navy. Nevertheless, as heir to the Cappoquin estate in 1892, it seems odd that instead of now returning home, Keane should have persisted with his military career for the next fifteen years. Following graduation from Woolwich, he was commissioned as a lieutenant in the Royal Field Artillery where he served for four years until 1896 when appointed aide-de-camp to George, fifth Earl Cadogan, Lord Lieutenant of Ireland 1895–1902, which at least allowed him to spend time each year in his native country. Already, during the period he had been based in England, he began to study law, and would eventually be called to the Bar in 1904, although he never practised as a barrister.

The outbreak of the second Boer War in October 1899 saw Keane return to the Royal Field Artillery and embark for South Africa, being promoted to the rank of captain during his time there, as well as receiving both the Queen's (Victoria) and King's (Edward VII) South African campaign medals. There were regular lulls between engagements, and Keane, forever curious and incapable of idleness, used these periods to investigate agricultural methods in that part of the world, and also to promote the co-operative movement, of which he was an ardent supporter. In January 1900 he noted in his diary that a local man to whom he had spoken about the movement, 'very much doubted when the principle of mutual self-help could be applied to the agricultural interests out here' since, it appeared, the Dutch settlers 'are anti-progress'.

On leaving South Africa, between 1902 and 1905 Keane was appointed private secretary to Sir Henry Blake, who having served as Governor of Hong Kong, had been appointed Governor of Ceylon (now Sri Lanka); on his eventual retirement in 1907, Blake and his wife would move to Myrtle Grove, the sixteenth-century unfortified house once owned by Sir Walter Raleigh and located in Youghal, twenty miles from Cappoquin.

During all the years Keane was engaged in military service and out of the country, the family estate had been managed on his behalf by his mother Adelaide and a land agent called Thomas Marmion. The latter often proved too conservative for Cappoquin's young owner, who thought Marmion 'lives very much in a groove and reluctantly accepts my new proposals'. Adelaide Keane, on the other hand, proved invaluable and indefatigable in taking care of her eldest son's best interests, right up to the time of her death in February 1907. The previous month she had been diagnosed with cancer and given only a short time to live. 'It is too terribly sad,' Keane wrote in his diary, 'a mother who has been everything in the world to her children, and now to see her dying slowly but surely before our eyes.' The end came sooner than expected, barely three weeks after the diagnosis.

The time had come for the Cappoquin estate's owner to assume full responsibility for his inheritance, and he resigned his army commission in June 1908. One reason for this is that by now he had become a husband and father. In fact, he had married the day after his mother's funeral (it was supposed to have taken place a couple of days earlier). His bride was Eleanor Hicks Beach, eldest child of Sir Michael Hicks Beach, a successful Conservative politician who served as Chancellor of the Exchequer and as Chief Secretary for Ireland on two occasions; in 1915 he was created first Earl St Aldwyn. The couple appear to have met first in May 1899 when Keane recorded in his diary, 'Miss Hicks Beach is a nice sort of girl.' Visiting her family a few days later, he judged them 'very nice kind simple people. Certain society would call them dull, the reason being they are not fast. They appear to have nice taste, to be well read, interested in what goes on around them.' The couple proved ideally matched, his wife having sufficient energy to keep up with Keane's many and varied activities. His energy, and curiosity, were almost boundless. In addition to the usual sports pursued by members of his class – hunting, shooting, polo – he played tennis, swam throughout the year in the Irish Sea when spending time in Dublin, keenly followed rugby and cricket, enjoyed cycling and would even walk from the railway station in Dungarvan to Cappoquin, a distance of some eleven miles. He enjoyed the theatre, opera and music, taking singing lessons for some time, participating in church choirs as well as performing at parties. Before the outbreak of the First World War, he served on Waterford County Council, was one of Lismore's Poor Law guardians, and in 1911 was Deputy Lieutenant and high sheriff of County Waterford. A regular churchgoer, he took an active role in the general synod of the Church of Ireland and was a member of the Representative Church Body.

A man of high principles, in May 1897 Keane had written in his diary: 'I hope to try and establish as my guiding factor throughout my public life; my country and the welfare of my people first and principles and standards of public honesty first ... Thus and thus alone can any man do justice to both his public and private morals.' He had long been interested in agricultural improvement, inspired by the work of Sir Horace Plunkett, advocate and founder of the co-operative movement in Ireland. He and Plunkett spent time together in 1897, when he wrote 'all we want is good men to organise and gather what can be gained by observing the experience of other countries far more advanced in their modes of agriculture than ourselves'. Within two year, Keane had become one of those men, determined to establish a co-operative in Cappoquin. Inevitably he encountered opposition, not least from the local parish priest and local newspaper the *Waterford Star*, the latter accusing Keane of trying to crush his local tenants. But his persistence paid off and by 1914 he had become secretary of the Blackwater Valley Co-Operative Agricultural Society Limited and had played a key role in the establishment of a co-operative bacon factory in Waterford, overseeing its construction and acting as its chairman. Several years earlier, in 1909, he attended the Royal Agricultural College, Cirencester to take a course in estate management – and then wrote a critique of the course. In September 1913 he went on a tour of Germany organized by the Royal English Arboricultural Society, commenting that the host country's 'systematic management is a very striking feature' and how he 'longed to give my fellow county councillors a sight of such things'. Unlike his ancestors, Keane was not given to enjoying a life of ease.

He brought a similar vigour to his family home, which he and his wife undertook to modernize, not least by installing a private acetylene lighting plant on the estate in 1910. Three years later they embarked on renovation work to the house, employing a young architect called Page Lawrence Dickinson. Today best recalled as co-author with Thomas Sadleir of *Georgian Mansions in Ireland* (1915) and as the nostalgic memorialist of *The Dublin of Yesterday* (1929), Dickinson was a son of the Dean of the Chapel Royal, Dublin. Around 1900 he had been apprenticed to the architectural practice of Richard Caulfield Orpen (an older brother of painter William Orpen). The two men subsequently entered into partnership as Orpen & Dickinson with offices on Dublin's South Frederick Street and it was during this period that Keane invited the firm's junior partner to devise schemes for the decoration of Cappoquin House's drawing room and for a new porch on the building's west side to replace one of wood or iron erected in the nineteenth century. The first task saw Dickinson design elaborate rococo plasterwork panels for the drawing room's walls, which were then made by Dublin contractor Michael Creedon and installed during spring 1914. Dickinson's handsome pedimented porch of cement-rendered concrete was a more substantial affair than its predecessor, sufficiently solid to have withstood the fire of 1923.

Perhaps further improvements to the house might have been undertaken, had not war broken out in August 1914. Six years after resigning his commission but still a member of the Officers' Reserve, Keane, now aged forty-one, returned to the army and was soon on his way to France, and then Belgium. Experiencing trench warfare at first hand and caught up in the Battle of Ypres that autumn, he wrote regularly to his wife, on one occasion telling her, 'I hear the town of Ypres, one of the finest in Flanders and full of gems of architecture, is flat. The destruction of warfare is appalling.' Since he was a friend of Geoffrey Dawson, then-editor of *The Times*, he was also able to give the newspaper's readers an idea of modern warfare, publishing a series of accounts under the title 'From the front: an artillery captain's journal of the war.' Yet despite the immediate horrors, he did not forget life back home. 'They make very good lace in Ypres,' he advised Eleanor in April 1915, 'and I must try and get you some, but there is a great run on it, and prices have doubled.' Nevertheless, the following day he wrote, 'I am sending you some lace which I bought this morning.'

It was a thoughtful gesture at a time when Eleanor Keane, like her late mother-in-law, had perforce assumed responsibility not just for looking after the couple's children and running the house but also managing the Cappoquin estate, with the requirement from her husband that she send him regular updates of what was happening. Little escaped his attention: as had been the case in South Africa, he made notes of local farming methods and how they might be applied in Ireland, informing Eleanor in February 1915 that he was busy writing an account of the operations of a typical Belgian farm for the Co-Operative Society's magazine *Homestead*: 'I have pumped the owner of this farm dry and am giving details of his crops, his labour, his stock, how he lives, a kind of Arthur Young inquiry which may be of interest at home.' Meanwhile, he was also instructing her on what to do back at home, writing the same month, 'I hope careful consideration will be given to the question of next year's crops. It might be advisable to grow rather more grain – possibly some wheat – than our working plan normally contemplates.'

Later that year and through 1916 he was responsible for instructing young officers in the use of new trench mortars, being promoted to major and awarded a Distinguished Service Order. During this period, news of the Easter Rising reached him, and he wrote home, 'They seem to have had a lot of fighting in Dublin. I imagine the rebels were full of drink. I see they looted shops in the most wholescale manner. The authorities seem to have been entirely unprepared at which I am not surprised.' But his wife was likely to have had other preoccupations since at precisely this time her only brother was killed in action in Egypt.

The following year, 1917, Keane moved to London to work on weapons development at the War Office, remaining there for the rest of the hostilities and ending his time with the rank of lieutenant colonel; he was also awarded the Légion d'honneur by the French government. Finally, he returned to civilian life in March 1919. 'I am looking forward with great joy to joining my family on Tuesday,' he told Eleanor. 'I feel I do not really know any of them now. Whatever the future may produce let us turn the present to best account.'

Doing so would prove a greater challenge than Keane probably realized. With his enquiring mind and abundant energy, he had always taken an interest in politics, harbouring ambitions as a young man to become a Member of Parliament. In April 1899 he wrote in his diary of feeling 'more confident than ever that I should be satisfied with my career if I was in the House of Commons, but how to get there is the difficulty. Yet one can generally achieve anything on which one sets one's mind.' Yet just a few months later, he admitted to himself, 'If I had to make up my mind tomorrow in which interest to stand for Parliament I would be in such difficulty that I am glad the opportunity not present.' Initially he seems to have been inclined to support the Conservative Party, but within a short time had begun to favour the Liberals. In August 1899, while staying at Haddo, the Scottish home of the Earl of Aberdeen, who had briefly served as Lord Lieutenant of Ireland in 1886 (and would do so again for ten years from 1905 onwards), he was urged by his forceful hostess to stand as a radical, she herself admitting to be in favour of Home Rule.

For many years Keane wavered between favouring the same course (in a letter to the editor of the *Irish Times* in February 1913, he declared 'I am a strong believer in Home Rule') and supporting the cause of Unionism. He was always conscious of the wrongs inflicted by an outside authority on his own country, on one occasion noting that laws had been instituted in Ireland 'by a class differing in religion, nationality, and sympathy and working in complete disregard of the people'. Yet he believed harmony and reconciliation were possible, 'but only by time and prudence, by considerate legislation and by due regard to the national character on the part of Englishmen who may be sent to this country to represent imperial government'. When elected to Waterford County Council in 1911, he became associated with William O'Brien's recently established All-for-Ireland League. O'Brien was a nationalist MP who had been instrumental in guiding the 1903 Wyndham Land Act to successful conclusion and would argue in favour of Ireland being granted Dominion status like that enjoyed by Canada. As a landlord one might have expected Keane not to share common interests with such a figure, but his abiding concern was always for the welfare of Ireland, and for the betterment of the country he and his ancestors had for many hundreds of years called home.

Sustaining that concern would not be easy over the years ahead. Just a month before he returned to Ireland in March 1919, the Sinn Féin republican party, which had won a majority of parliamentary seats in the previous December's general election, established its own breakaway government and declared Ireland's independence from Britain. Armed conflict between Irish and British forces gradually spread across the country. While inevitably this had an impact on Cappoquin and the Blackwater region, a more immediate concern for Keane was dealing with trouble on his own farm. During the closing years of the war, agricultural labourers had begun to organize themselves and to campaign for improved wages. In the Waterford region, a Land and Labour Union was formed in 1917, before being absorbed into the Irish Transport and General Workers Union, which by 1919 had established a branch in Cappoquin; by the following year the majority of farm labourers in this part of the country were members of the union. As they demanded improved pay, their employers, faced in the aftermath of the war with falling prices for agricultural produce, sought a reduction in wages. Farmers large and small now formed their own accredited body, the Irish Farmers' Union, which by 1920 had 60,000 members across Ireland. Representing the IFU in that part of the country, the Waterford Farmers' Association had thirty-one branches, and was chaired by Keane. From the start he adopted a pugnacious response to the workers and their claims, refusing to negotiate with union officials and establishing a strike-breaking force. Inevitably this led to local conflict and by early 1922, to open hostilities as workers began to raid farms and halt their activity. Cappoquin was not immune from such activity. In early June 1922, Keane noted in his diary, 'I heard that pickets had arrived at farm. I went up and found a dozen pickets men there ... Told them they had no authority to enter my place ... they already had the farm men on the road. They then went and by threats but no actual violence got out the garden men.' Within days other workers on the estate were called out and its operations risked coming to a halt. The new Free State government, already fighting the anti-Treaty forces and anxious that agricultural activity across the country should not come to a halt, was largely supportive of the farmers. Keane travelled to Dublin and there met Minister for Lands and Agriculture Patrick Hogan, who he described as 'sympathetic and angry, took notes and said he would see the minister for defence [Richard Mulcahy]. He took a gloomy view of things.' But while away from Cappoquin, Keane was informed by his wife that fifteen cattle had been taken from the farm (they were recovered three days later in Clonmel, County Tipperary). Circumstances did not improve and soon he was writing to his solicitor asking that an application for compensation be

made to the government since, he claimed, members of the ITGWU
had taken over his dairy, milked the cattle 'and have sold + retained
the proceeds'. By the middle of the month, he wondered if he would
have to sell the herd, thereby leaving the area without milk for the
winter. Soon afterwards he received a letter threatening violence and
his telephone line was cut. Understandably, a note of despondency
now enters his diary as he despaired of his fellow members of the
IFU, concluding 'farmers as a whole inert and avaricious and they
will get it in the neck before things are right'. However, early the
following month a settlement in the area was negotiated and workers
on the Cappoquin estate returned to their jobs, Keane noting, 'The
men came down to yard at 1.00 [am]. They all went back to work.
So the strike is over and I do not think I have lost very much.' He
had been particularly pleased with the firm support received from the
government, later declaring:

> were it not for the protection afforded by the armed forces of the
> State, a bitter class war might have been precipitated. The action
> of the government in affording protection in a firm and impartial
> manner, and thus establishing the principle that any who wish to
> work unmolested, is a good omen for the future of the State.

The decisive support provided by government agencies may have
encouraged Keane in December 1922 to take up the offer of a seat in
the Senate, the upper chamber of the new state's legislature. In a house
of sixty members, he was one of the thirty nominated by William
T. Cosgrave, President of the Executive Council. Most of the others
in this group were, like Keane, landowners and former southern
unionists, including seven peers and five baronets. The majority of
them had been accustomed to sitting on councils and committees,
and to devoting at least some of their time to public service. All of
them now became targets for anti-Treaty supporters, who sought to
intimidate Senate members, not least by attacking – and too frequently

destroying – their homes: out of sixty senators, thirty-seven would have their properties burnt.

House burnings had, of course, been a feature of the War of Independence, and many owners accordingly had taken precautions. As early as September 1921, just months after ceasefire between British and Irish forces had been declared, Keane was in touch with furniture companies seeking quotes for the cost of removing the more valuable contents from Cappoquin. Initially these items were placed in storage before being brought to London where his wife and their four children had already moved for reasons of safety. The partial emptying of his home led Keane to question whether he would remain in the country: 'I do feel this is the beginning of our family's severance with Ireland.' By the end of February 1922, two vanloads of furniture and pictures, plate, china and glass had been taken away although a lot of other larger items remained in the house, not least the contents of the library. Some of this was intended for nearby Tivoli, a dower house, because Keane now contemplated letting Cappoquin, although he insisted, 'I will not consider any other than a first class tenant of good social and financial standing who will appreciate and respect the place.'

No such tenant was forthcoming, and Cappoquin House, left only semi-furnished and scarcely occupied, looked increasingly vulnerable to attack. Indeed, a month before it was burnt, a number of Irish newspapers carried an erroneous report that this had happened, as by then had already been the case with the residences of Keane's friends and Senate colleagues John Bagwell (Marlfield, County Tipperary) and Sir Horace Plunkett (Kilteragh, County Dublin), in both instances with the total loss of valuable contents. A fortnight before Cappoquin's destruction, Keane had noted in his diary, 'daily reports from Ireland of burning houses: ours must go in time'. And go it did, on the night of 19 February 1923. Since the building was unoccupied at the time, there were no witnesses to the attack, and by the time the fire was noticed it had already taken hold. Miss Bell, who worked in the estate office, walked up from the village to the house in the early hours of the morning and reported, 'when I arrived there the principal part of the front and back block was a blazing furnace, the roof gone and all the lofts and windows, with the exception of the two at the west end over the portico'.

In the aftermath of Cappoquin House's burning, Keane displayed his customary vigour and decisiveness: within days, he had not only instructed his solicitor to seek compensation from the Free State government, but also made contact with Page L Dickinson, the architect responsible for work on the building ten years earlier. By then, however, Dickinson had moved to England and was living in Harrogate, Yorkshire. While willing to advise on the cost of the house's reconstruction, estimated in May 1923 to be £31,200, less £7800 provided the building's old walls were retained, Dickinson felt unable to offer any further services and therefore proposed his erstwhile partner as supervisory architect.

In December 1923 Keane offered Orpen the job, his fee being 5 per cent of whatever compensation award was made by the government. In fact, when Orpen drew up a final claim the following March it was lower than that earlier proposed by Dickinson, the total anticipated cost now being £16,253, seventeen shillings and one penny (again including retention of the old walls). Despite Keane's prompt request for compensation, it was not until May 1924 that a decision was made on the amount to be awarded for damage to Cappoquin House and the final figure was a disappointing £12,000. In addition, he received £800 for the loss of furniture and £160, nine shillings and threepence for costs and expenses. Securing the money proved as slow a process for him as it did for many other owners of houses similarly damaged during the Civil War. The funds were paid out in stages over a number of years and only in response to persistent requests for reimbursement in the aftermath of expenditure. While the first cheque for £1500 was sent in January 1925, the final instalment (for £900) appears to have been paid in December 1930, by which date the greater part of work on the house had long since been completed.

That work began in September 1924 with the installation of concrete beams above which was placed a flat concrete roof with a single opening for the glazed dome over the house's main staircase, the task overseen by the Dublin engineering firm of Delap & Waller. The decision to give the building a flat rather than pitched roof proved unwise: even by 1927 it had begun to show cracks and a long history of unsatisfactory repairs lay ahead. Other sections of the building's restoration were more successful, aided by close supervision on the parts of Keane and his wife, both of whom engaged in extensive correspondence with Orpen over every detail of the project. Typically, at the end of July 1928, Sir John wrote to the architect: 'I am returning your drawings of the proposed arrangement for the library. My wife and I have talked over the matter and think it would be better if the face of the plaster over the fireplace came out flush with the front of the upper portion of the bookcases.'

While the greater part of the labour force was local, a lot of the material used in the house's restoration, whether sanitary ware or wood for flooring, came from England. Perhaps Creedon of Dublin was no longer in business, but the task of creating new plasterwork decoration for the main rooms was given to the London firm of G Jackson & Sons. That for the dining room cost £74 while the north hall's plasterwork cost just £1 less. The latter, which opens into the yard, now became the main entrance, this realignment of the house being the most significant change made by Orpen. The south hall, previously used as an entrance, was turned into a drawing room, Jackson & Sons billing the Keanes £284 for its elaborate plaster decoration including the screen of columns and pilasters. Ultimately shortage of funds meant that the original drawing room, decorated in 1914 with splendid rococo-style plasterwork, had to be left with its walls and ceiling plain: it became a billiard room.

It was essential Cappoquin House be fully habitable by the start of January 1930 since the Keanes then held a dance on the premises for over 150 guests to mark the twenty-first birthday of their son Richard.

His father was then still a senator, and remained so until 1934 when he failed to win re-election. However, when the modern Seanad Éireann was established by the Constitution of Ireland in 1937, Keane was offered a place by then-Taoiseach Éamon de Valera, somewhat surprisingly since the two men had little in common. Keane continued to serve as a senator until 1944, and four years earlier was also nominated to the first Council of State. He was frequently described as a maverick, and a profile published in September 1925 observed that he took 'a positive delight in tilting at popular idols and ideals' and 'never fails to remind us in his speeches that he represents a minority'. Keane was then leading opposition to the proposed Shannon Electrification Scheme, believing, he explained, that there had been 'no proper consideration of alternative schemes; no proper reference to experts; no power of revising estimates and that estimates were not binding'. He was also known for his opposition to censorship: in November 1942, following the banning of Eric Cross's book *The Tailor and Ansty*, he proposed a motion of no confidence in the role of the Censorship of Publications Board, and read a number of passages from the novel in the Senate Chamber. The subsequent public record drily noted, 'The Senator quoted from the book.' He died in January 1958 at the age of eighty-two. A rare instance of a family home fully resurrected after the Troubles, Cappoquin House is now home to the seventh baronet, Sir Charles Keane.

7

'I had to escape and leave the country'
BARBAVILLA AND CLONYN CASTLE,
COUNTY WESTMEATH

ON 4 APRIL 1882 the *Irish Times* carried the first of what would be many reports about an incident that had occurred two days earlier in County Westmeath. It was, wrote the newspaper's Special Reporter, 'one of the foulest and most dastardly murders which have for many years been committed in Ireland ... amid every attendant circumstance which could attach the utmost guilt to the crime, and invest the fearful outrage with the most horrible character'. On the morning of 2 April William Barlow Smythe, owner of the Barbavilla estate, had attended church in the nearby village of Collinstown, accompanied by his sister-in-law Maria Smythe and her two daughters, as well as Lady Harriet Monck, sister of his late wife. As the carriage returned back to the house, a shot was fired from within a clump of trees on one side of the avenue. Presumably intended for Barbavilla's owner, the discharged bullet instead hit Mrs Smythe in the back of the head, killing her instantly. Among the disturbances of the period's Land Wars, this – the murder of an innocent woman as she returned from church – was one that caused perhaps the most widespread public shock and revulsion.

The Smythes of Barbavilla could trace their origins back to the first half of the seventeenth century when one Ralph Smyth, a tanner based in Lisburn, County Antrim, began buying up various debentures and allotments from Cromwellian soldiers who in lieu of pay had been given land confiscated from the native Irish. In this way, according to a later family record, 'Ralph became the owner of land and property apart from his own at Ballymacash, although not all of this property was confiscated from the "Rebbells".' Indeed, he acquired so much land and property that aside from Viscount Conway's castle, he possessed the largest establishment in the Lisburn area, having built himself a fine house on its own grounds. Ralph Smyth had a number of sons, one of whom, William, became an Anglican clergyman and steadily rose through the clerical ranks before finally being appointed Bishop of Kilmore. He also married well: his wife Mary was the daughter of Sir John Povey, an English-born lawyer who ended as Lord Chief Justice of Ireland.

Like his father before him, William Smyth bought up parcels of land, especially in County Westmeath, which was soon populated with branches of the family living on a number of estates including Drumcree, Glananea and Gaybrook. The Manor and Castle of Ranaghan were among his acquisitions, bought for £1100 in 1670. This property had formerly belonged to the Luttrell family, who forfeited the land for their part in the Confederate Wars of the 1640s. In due course the bishop settled this estate on his third son, likewise called William. He also bequeathed William nearby Lough Lene running to 889 acres. Again, like his father and grandfather William Smyth junior married well in 1713, his wife being Barbara, daughter of Colonel Sir George Ingoldsby, an English soldier who had come to Ireland with his cousin Oliver Cromwell, and sister of General Richard Ingoldsby who amassed a sufficient fortune to buy Carton, County Kildare (formerly and subsequently belonging to the FitzGeralds, Earls of Kildare). Unfortunately, General Ingoldsby's son Henry quickly ran through much of his inheritance – Carton eventually had to be sold – before he died in 1731, leaving two daughters. William Smyth, married to their great-aunt, acted as one of the girls' guardians. Nevertheless, despite his care and despite their reduced wealth, in 1743 one of the girls, Frances Ingoldsby, was abducted by the fortune hunter Hugh Fitzjohn

Massy. A reward was placed on Massy's head, so he – and his bride – fled to France, only returning home the following year by which time Frances was expecting her first child.

For the first part of her own marriage, Frances's aunt Barbara lived with William Smyth in the Dublin district of Stoneybatter but around 1732 the couple began constructing a country residence for themselves on the Ranaghan estate. Like many gentlemen of the period, William, who would sweetly rename the property Barbavilla in honour of his wife, dabbled in architecture, and was responsible for designing a number of buildings, not least his own new home; it probably helped that his sister Mary had married Ireland's Surveyor-General Thomas Burgh, responsible for such significant buildings as the library in Trinity College and Steevens's Hospital, both in Dublin. William drew on his brother-in-law for assistance, and set aside £2000 for the construction of Barbavilla. As a result, already, by 1733 one of the Smyths' neighbours in County Westmeath, Sir Richard Levinge, could describe their new home as 'a delightful villa ... in that small, enchanted spot'. While her husband played amateur architect, Barbara Smyth took particular trouble over the gardens around the house, writing to William during one of his absences, 'I am in more pain for this piece of management than any other you ever enjoined me to.' Alas, Barbavilla's chatelaine did not have much time to enjoy her handiwork, dying just a few years later in 1738.

Considerably enlarged towards the end of the eighteenth century and further altered in the nineteenth, Barbavilla was originally a house of two storeys over raised basement and of six bays. The building was slightly old-fashioned for the period, showing little awareness of newer trends in domestic design and suggesting that William Smyth possessed more enthusiasm than real talent. On the other hand, as an inventory of Barbavilla's contents compiled 1742–6 demonstrates, he was very proud of his new home and filled it with the best that he could afford, not least a mahogany cabinet-on-stand incorporating a Florentine pietra dura cabinet; this may have been purchased for him by his brother the Rev. James Smyth, who had travelled to Italy.

Following its builder's death, successive generations of the family followed in Barbavilla, alternating the first name Ralph and William until 1815 when following the premature death of his father, William Barlow Smythe inherited Barbavilla at the age of six: the main achievement of his deceased parent appears to have been the addition of an 'e' to the end of the family name. Until he reached his majority in 1830, the young heir's affairs were managed by his uncle, Henry Meade Smythe. In due course he assumed responsibility for his own affairs and in 1837 married Lady Emily Monck, one of the nine daughters of Henry Monck, first (and last) Earl of Rathdowne who lived at Charleville outside Enniskerry in County Wicklow. Lady Emily's mother, Lady Frances Trench, was an admirer of the Reverend Robert Daly, an evangelical Church of Ireland clergyman notorious for his hatred of Roman Catholicism. Daly eventually rose to become Bishop of Cashel and Waterford, and was judged to have assumed 'the position and bearing of a Protestant pope'. William Barlow Smythe likewise became a supporter of evangelical Christianity, which led him into difficulties with the Catholic clergy in his own part of Westmeath but it is understandable that he should have sought religious consolation since his wife died within nine months of their wedding after giving birth to the couple's only child, a daughter also named Emily. In 1842 the little girl, then aged five, also died, leaving her father a solitary widower.

It was forty years later, in 1882, that Maria Smythe was killed as she and other members of the family returned to the house after attending Palm Sunday services in Collinstown. At some time earlier, William Barlow Smythe had for the first time evicted one of his tenants, Richard Riggs, on the grounds of persistent non-payment of rent on a 67-acre farm. Riggs was not held to have been responsible for the murder of Mrs Smythe. Indeed, the man believed to have fired the shot emigrated to the United States while, following a two-year police investigation, ten local farmers were convicted of conspiracy to murder, five of them sentenced to ten years in prison, five of them to seven years. By now aged seventy-three, William Barlow Smythe no longer wished to remain in Ireland, handing over responsibility for the estate to an agent while he moved to Ilfracombe, Devon, where he died in 1886.

Barbavilla was inherited by his younger brother Henry, husband of the murdered Maria Smythe. Through his mother, Eliza Lyster, he had inherited New Park, an estate in County Roscommon, but the house there had been badly damaged by fire in 1860 and the property was sold, perhaps because by then Henry knew he was heir to Barbavilla. However, following his wife's murder and his brother's death, and by then also in his mid-seventies, he passed responsibility for the Westmeath estate to his eldest son, Colonel William Lyster-Smythe. The colonel had served time in the army before becoming Assistant Private Secretary to Earl Spencer when the latter was Lord Lieutenant of Ireland 1882–5, then Gentleman-in-Waiting to a number of Spencer's successors before being appointed aide-de-camp in 1906 to the Earl of Aberdeen when he became Lord Lieutenant for a second period.

On his death in April 1920 Colonel Lyster-Smythe left his entire estate not, as might have been expected, to his eldest son Henry Ingoldsby Lyster-Smythe. The latter had married Elizabeth Palæmona Unger-Vetlesen, daughter of a Norwegian surgeon and private physician to King Oscar II (much later she would establish a medical fund in her father's memory). It appears his father did not approve of their son's choice of bride, and so he was cut out of the will, Barbavilla being left instead to the colonel's widow, Agnes. She much preferred her second-born, Cecil St George Lyster-Smythe, who during the war had served as a captain in the Royal Flying Corps. At the time of his father's death, he was in Egypt (where another son, Richard, the youngest, had drowned the previous year while bathing at Jaffa) acting as second-in-command of Intelligence at GHQ Cairo. In May 1921, owing to injuries received during his time in the RFC, he retired on half-pay with the intention of returning to live with his mother in Ireland. However, as he later explained in a document seeking compensation for damage to the family property, the situation in the country at the time was such that he was felt unable even to visit: 'There was a War Office order preventing men or officers going to Ireland.' In September 1922 he decided to investigate matters for himself, 'but about 100-120 Republicans seized the house (Barbavilla House) while I was in it, and I had to escape and leave the country'. This was something of an exaggeration on the captain's part. What actually happened was that a number of anti-Treaty supporters took over the building and, after two days' occupation, found themselves under attack by Free State troops, 'fully equipped and having a machine gun'. According to a report in the *Westmeath Examiner*:

> A fierce and hot engagement ensued, the machine gun being called into action. Eventually the Irregulars hastily evacuated, taking to the dense and extensive woods of the estate, from which for some time they kept up spasmodic firing at the National troops ... The front of Barbavilla House, and the windows and glass bear plain evidence of the attack and conflict.

Under these circumstances, Captain Lyster-Smythe's departure from the family home is understandable. He came back once more in October 1923. Still finding conditions too volatile and believing himself unsafe, he left again, only returning for good in March 1925. As a result of his absences, Captain Lyster-Smythe contended, he was unable to secure his property. Furthermore, 'my agent had been burnt out of two houses and himself subjected to great persecutions, so that no notification of the injuries could be sent to me'.

Those 'injuries' were inflicted on a building rather than a person: a bungalow standing on the shores of Lough Lene. Originally constructed in 1890 as a fishing lodge, the building was entirely looted in January

1921, and an adjacent boathouse containing a steel vessel 'was badly damaged and the zinc removed off the walls and roof, the boat had a hole put in it, and the engine was smashed up'. Its owner therefore applied to the Irish Grants Committee for financial redress: £150 for the bungalow, and £85 for the boathouse and boat. The application was only made in November 1926, by which time the claimant was settled at Barbavilla, but not happy, finding himself obliged to live on a modest military pension of £180 per annum, plus an allowance of £120 from his mother 'and a 5% commission on work done for her in connection with the estate, about another £50'. For an ex-army officer in his thirties, a yearly income of £350 (the equivalent of £22,500 in 2022) could hardly be considered satisfactory, and it is understandable that Captain Lyster-Smythe sought financial redress for the losses he had suffered.

However, the matter did not end there. In July 1927 he submitted an amended claim to the grants committee, one in which the sums had increased substantially. While the amount sought for repair of the boathouse and boat remained £85, the bungalow and its contents were deemed to be worth £188. In addition, £250 was requested as compensation for the captain's inability to use the property over the previous five years, due to its damaged state. Furthermore, it transpired that two other buildings owned by the family in Collinstown – the courthouse and schoolhouse – had similarly been attacked and looted during the period 1921–2: in total, £400 was requested by the captain for the damage to these and consequent loss of income due to lack of rental. He then asked for £450 as compensation for being unable to live in Barbavilla for three years, and £600 to pay for 'expenses for removal from Ireland twice and extra expense of living away, four years'. Captain Lyster-Smythe's original request had been for £235; it had now swollen to £3373. The largest single figure was a claim for £1020 arising from eighty-five acres of the estate's best land which, he explained, he had been unable to farm for a number of years, even though obliged to pay rates of £180 over the same period. This parcel of land, known as Lake Farm, had been seized by an elderly woman living in an adjacent cottage, Ellen Riggs. She was a daughter of Richard Riggs, the tenant whose non-payment of rent back in 1882 had led to his eviction and so to the shooting of Maria Smythe. Ellen Riggs claimed she had a right to the land as her father had been unfairly deprived of it. In 1921 and in the absence of Captain Lyster-Smythe, she had seized possession of the property and the following year offered it for sale through a local auctioneer: the latter, on being informed by Barbavilla's agent that Miss Riggs had no legal right to the land, had withdrawn from the matter.

Meanwhile, the agent, burnt out of two houses, had left the area. A new one was duly appointed, but he was based in Nenagh, County Tipperary, some eighty miles south-west of Collinstown and therefore not able to ensure Barbavilla's security. In consequence, Captain Lyster-Smythe also being absent until March 1925, Miss Riggs had persisted in her claim and any time a lock was placed on the gate leading to the land and cattle put on the land, she broke it and drove off the cattle. Finally, in May 1925 the matter went to court where Miss Riggs, who preferred to represent herself, declared that she was the legal owner of the land and would persist in her behaviour. When the judge tried to reason with her, warned of fines and even imprisonment, and set a bond of £5 to keep the peace, she responded, 'It does not matter about any bond. If Smythe's cattle are put on these lands, the lock will go again.' The Irish Land Commission embarked on an investigation into the matter but it seems not to have been satisfactorily resolved as late as July 1927 when Captain Lyster-Smythe submitted his revised claim of £3373 to the Irish Grants Committee.

Two months later he wrote to the that organization, enquiring when his application would be considered and whether he might be given an interim grant: in November he received £250 provisional payment. A further £375 followed before, in February 1928, the captain's solicitors were told that the committee had decided to give him total compensation of £1000, meaning a sum of £375 remained outstanding. While this was less than a third of the amount sought, the committee noted that Captain Lyster-Smythe had not owned Barbavilla when most of the outrages occurred. In a letter accompanying his application, he had explained, 'In March 1924 my mother who was left the property, made over to me the Mansion House of Barbavilla, together with all untenanted lands, or lands not included in the Irish Lands Act.' Attached to the letter was a copy of a legal document, signed by his mother at the British Consulate in Nice in March 1924, which appeared to confirm that the property at Barbavilla had indeed been given to him. However, it also confirmed that transfer of ownership occurred only after much of the damage, and consequent loss of income, had taken place. Hence the committee decided £1000 was sufficient recompense.

There the matter ought to have ended, but the following year, in September 1929, the Irish Grants Committee received a letter from Captain Lyster-Smythe's mother Agnes, asking what monies had been paid to her son. Despite the favouritism she had always shown him, it transpired he had not reciprocated by looking after his parent's best interests. Nor, when it came to ownership of the Barbavilla estate, had he accurately represented himself to the committee. 'I may state,' his mother now explained, 'that this property belongs absolutely to me, as it was left to me by my husband, the late Colonel Lyster Smythe. I trusted my son to act for me and I allowed him to have compensation granted to me for the house, as he undertook to have the damage rectified.' However, she added, there had been no agreement between her and her son that he should receive money given in compensation for loss of income on the lands and, as a result, 'I am now anxious to know what you can do in the matter for me.'

The answer from a representative of the committee was that it could do very little. While acknowledging that an unstated percentage of the grant made to Captain Lyster-Smythe was for loss of income from the eighty-five acres which had been the subject of a legal dispute with Ellen Riggs, 'the Irish Grants Committee are unable to intervene between Captain Smythe and yourself in the question as to what part, if any, of the total award should be allocated in respect of your interest in the property'. Not surprisingly, this response failed to satisfy Agnes Lyster-Smythe, and she soon wrote back saying her son had not had any power of attorney to represent her in any dealings with the committee, and while the document of March 1924 may have given him responsibility for the house and untenanted land, 'it gave him neither possession nor control of my farm lands, of which the 85 acres form a part, during my lifetime, as can be proved'. As far as she was concerned, this was 'a case of mismanagement, pure and simple, & I intend to have the matter dealt with accordingly'. In November her elder son Ingoldsby Lyster-Smythe, despite any differences he had with his mother, was prevailed upon to write to the committee, laying out many of the same points as had Agnes, and arguing that before any money was paid out more investigation should have been undertaken into who owned what property. 'No doubt your Committee will consider the advisability of reopening the matter with Cecil St. George Lyster-Smythe,' he concluded, 'and in the meantime, Mrs Lyster-Smythe will lodge with you a claim for compensation for her Lake Farm for consideration by your Committee.'

He got no more satisfaction than had Agnes. The same committee representative informed Ingoldsby Lyster-Smythe that at the hearing of the claim, his brother, attended by a solicitor and counsel, had claimed to be entitled to any compensation made and, after the case had been given all due consideration, the monies had been discharged through the same solicitor. Having already paid out money, the committee had no intention of entertaining a second claim from the Barbavilla estate. Politely, but firmly, it was recommended 'that you should negotiate with Captain Lyster-Smythe as to the distribution of the total award.'

The widowed Agnes had, it seems, been defrauded by her favourite son, and there was nothing she could do about it. Nor did he mend his ways before eventually dying in the south of France in 1948. His mother outlived him by four years, and when she died, ownership of Barbavilla finally passed to the only remaining member of the family, the decent but ill-used Henry Ingoldsby Lyster-Smythe. By then, however, there was no money left to support the place and so in September 1954 the house and 542 acres of land was sold. The following June, Barbavilla's contents, many of which had been in the property since it had been built more than 200 years before, were dispersed at auction over the course of four days. One of those pieces was the exceedingly rare cabinet-on-stand incorporating a Florentine pietra dura cabinet; where this valuable piece of furniture went is unknown. Today Barbavilla is a goat farm.

Less than ten kilometres to the east of Barbavilla is the small town of Delvin. It provided the setting for a novel published in 1918. *The Valley of the Squinting Windows* was written by Brinsley MacNamara (1890–1963), a pseudonym of John Weldon whose father James was principal of a national school elsewhere in the county. Owing more to nineteenth-century melodrama than twentieth-century realism, and closer in spirit to *Peyton Place* than to *Madame Bovary*, the book caused a huge stir in the area when it first appeared: outraged at this fictional portrayal, the denizens of Delvin publicly burnt a copy in the centre of the town. Worse, they organized a boycott of children attending the school run by MacNamara's father, as though he were responsible for his son's novel. (In response, James Weldon brought a law suit for £4000 against Delvin's parish priest and seven parishioners for arranging the prohibition. He lost the case and was forced to emigrate.)

MacNamara's mistake was to make the inspiration for his fictional town so easily identifiable, not least thanks to several references in the novel to the remains of a large Norman castle at one end of the town. Just such a castle can still be seen in Delvin, thought to have been built in the late twelfth century by Sir Gilbert de Nogent, a Norman knight who had come to Ireland in the company of his father-in-law, Hugh de Lacy. When Henry II granted de Lacy the Lordship of Meath, the latter in turn gave de Nogent the barony of Delvin, and so the family, who in due course became Nugent, settled down in this part of the country. In the late forteenth century William Fitzrichard Nugent was created the first Baron Delvin and thereafter one generation followed another until 1621 when Richard Nugent was created Earl of Westmeath. A few years later, as though to mark his elevation, he abandoned the Norman castle for a new residence, Clonyn Castle, a little to the north of the town. Barely had work on this been completed than it was gutted by fire, seemingly on the instructions of the earl's grandson who, in the aftermath of the sacking of Drogheda in September 1649, feared the building might fall into the hands of the advancing Cromwellian army. For his pains, he was subsequently deprived of his property and banished to Connacht, but once Charles II was restored to the throne in 1660, he received his land back, along with a generous pension. The second earl then rebuilt his grandfather's castle, which intermittently served as a residence for the family until the third quarter of the nineteenth century. In the second half of the eighteenth century, the building was greatly enlarged, becoming a long, two-storey house with a full-height bow at one end.

Throughout this period, the Nugents were resolutely Roman Catholic. The third Earl of Westmeath, for example, was a Capuchin friar in France and appears never to have assumed the title. He was succeeded by his younger brother Thomas Nugent, who, after supporting James II during the king's time in Ireland, was outlawed but then permitted to return to his estates under the terms of the Treaty of Limerick. Since neither of his sons married, he was in turn succeeded by another brother, John Nugent, who spent the greater part of his life as a professional soldier in the French army, ending his career in 1744 as a maréchal de camp. On his death a decade later, his son Thomas became the sixth earl. The latter, already living back in Ireland, conformed to the Established Church, the first of his family to do so. As a result, he was able to take his seat in the Irish Houses of Parliament, then becoming a Privy Councillor, Grandmaster of the Grand Lodge in Ireland and, in 1783, one of the founder knights of the Order of St Patrick.

Nevertheless, despite these outward trappings of social and political success, perhaps it might have been better had the family remained Catholic, because from the sixth earl onward misfortune stalked one generation after another. In August 1761 his heir Richard Nugent, Lord Delvin, apparently having consumed too much alcohol, offended a woman met in Dublin's then-fashionable Marlborough Green. The lady's companion challenged Lord Delvin to a duel in which the young man was killed. A later commentator on the incident reported, 'I have heard it said that little or no enquiry was ever made about the matter, as society found they could get on very well without Lord Delvin.' Indeed, the incident's only lasting consequence seems to have been that Marlborough Green fell out of fashion as a popular place of resort.

Lord Delvin's father, whose first wife died some time earlier, remarried and had a second son, George Frederick Nugent, who in 1792 became seventh Earl of Westmeath. His own personal life was not without some setbacks. In 1796 he sued the politician Augustus Cavendish-Bradshaw for 'criminal conversation', the term then used for adultery. Bradshaw, it transpired, had been having an affair with the countess (their trysts having taken place in Her Ladyship's carriage, and thus being observed by her coachman). In due course, Lord Westmeath was awarded £10,000, although it is open to question whether this was ever paid by the impoverished Cavendish-Bradshaw who did at least behave honourably and marry his now-divorced lover.

Within a year of the court case, the seventh earl had remarried and although he had several more children, it was a son of his first marriage who in 1814 became the next Lord Westmeath. Created Marquess of Westmeath eight years later, his marital life was even more unhappy than that of his father. In 1812 he married the wealthy Lady Emily Cecil, a daughter of the first Marquess of Salisbury: within a decade they separated and in 1827 Lady Westmeath was able to obtain a judicial separation but the couple never divorced (despite Lord Westmeath attempting to accuse his estranged wife of adultery with the Duke of Wellington, to whom she was related). Only after her death was the eighth earl free to marry again, which he did in 1858 at the age of seventy-two. This second marriage also ended badly: within four years Lord Westmeath was suing his wife for divorce on the grounds of adultery. Remarkably, in 1864 at the age of seventy-eight he married a third time and remained in this state until his death in 1871.

The Marquess of Westmeath had only one legitimate child, Lady Rosa Emily Nugent, who duly inherited the family estates. In 1840 she married Fulke Southwell Greville and, in deference to his father-in-law in 1866 he changed his surname to Greville-Nugent; three years later, he also acquired a peerage, becoming Lord Greville of Clonyn. By this time, the property from which he derived his title had fallen into serious disrepair, seemingly owing to its neglect by the marquess. Many years before, the latter's estranged wife remembered being abandoned by her husband in the old house in the depths of winter 'in a room not papered, sashes rotten … not allowed anything but green wood …' Accordingly, Lord Greville opted to have new residences built for himself both at Clonyn and elsewhere in the country at Clonhugh on a site overlooking Lough Owel. Whereas Clonhugh, designed by William Caldbeck, was a typical Victorian villa, Clonyn is something else altogether. An immense Gothic Revival castle, it was rightly described by the late Jeremy Williams as 'utterly humourless', and consists of a vast limestone block with identical circular towers at each corner and surrounded by a dry moat. Although architect John McCurdy (today remembered for having designed Dublin's Shelbourne Hotel) presumably meant to evoke medieval splendour, as Williams commented, 'any semblance to antiquity is dispelled by serried ranks of humdrum, round-arched, plate-glass windows that contrive to give this haughty pile a premonition of suburbia'. The interior is no better, a sequence of chilly, high-ceilinged rooms opening off a double-height entrance hall, this space dominated by a great stone staircase that leads to the first-floor bedroom gallery.

As so often, the owners of this rather pretentious monstrosity did not enjoy it for long. Lady Greville died in Boulogne in January 1883 and it was arranged that her body be brought back to Ireland for burial. The coffin travelled by train and boat to Dublin, and was then placed on another train and brought to Mullingar where it was put on a horse-drawn hearse. However, when the coachman and his assistant arrived at Clonyn Castle, they discovered the coffin was missing: en route to the house, it had slipped off the vehicle and was found lying on the side of the road (the coachman and his assistant, it transpired, had stopped for a drink or two on their way). The deceased being brought home at last, a burial duly took place and that same evening, Lord Greville dined with his three sons, after which he had a heart attack and died. That, at least, is how his demise was officially reported: unofficially it was said that he had quarrelled with his children who then pushed him down the stone staircase. Whatever the explanation, three days later he was reunited with his wife in her tomb.

If his sons fought with their father, it may have been over his arrangements for the estate. Lord Greville had vested Clonyn in a trust, with residency in the house being given not, as might have been expected, to the eldest son but to the youngest, Patrick Greville-Nugent with the proviso that, should he have no heir, the property would go to his sister Mildred, who in 1869 had married a French aristocrat, the Marquis de la Bédoyère. The two siblings soon found themselves at odds with each other, and in January 1890 Mme de la Bédoyère initiated legal proceedings against her brother, alleging that he had cut down many specimen trees on the Clonyn estate. Since she stood every chance of inheriting the estate (Patrick Greville-Nugent having no children), what took place there was of concern to her. After four months the High Court in Dublin found the castle's occupant had indeed been responsible for the felling of 12,000 larch, ash and sycamore trees, that his intention had been to make money from the sale of timber, and that he had no authority to engage in such activity. He was ordered to cease forthwith.

The case made public the Greville-Nugents' financial difficulties. The construction of Clonyn Castle, it transpired, had cost their father more than £30,000 with equally substantial sums spent at Clonhugh. Mortgages had been taken out and these now required repayment: in consequence, Patrick Greville-Nugent sought to make money whatever way he could. Gradually over the next decade or so, the greater part of the estate, which once ran to 10,000 acres, was sold under the terms of the Land Acts. By the start of the twentieth century, only the demesne remained, with Patrick Greville-Nugent annually given £750 by the trustees from surplus rents paid by tenants. It was only a matter of time before the final sale took place, and indeed in July 1919 Clonyn Castle and 1353 acres was put on the market. The land was bought for just over £25,000 by four trustees acting for a group of local people who planned to divide it into a number of small holdings. But no one wanted the castle, which in October 1919 had been offered to the county council for use as a tuberculosis dispensary: the offer was declined. The following March Clonyn Castle was advertised for sale with 135 acres: it was bought for £4000 by a local entrepreneur Patrick J. Weymes.

Born in Kinnegad, Weymes had inherited the family wool and tanning business, which he then greatly expanded, along the way becoming chairman of the United Irish League, chairman of Westmeath County Council and Commissioner of the Peace. In the 1918 General Election he had run for the Irish Parliamentary Party but came second after the Sinn Féin party, and thereafter his business affairs began to go badly awry. Given the increasingly precarious nature of his finances, the purchase of Clonyn Castle seems strange, unless he was hoping for a quick resale from which he might make a profit. In May 1921 he put the place on the market but there were no buyers; at the time, there was little interest in the acquisition of large country houses in Ireland.

Clonyn Castle sat empty and neglected until early March 1923 when a group of men attacked the building and started a fire on the premises. Within a few days, Weymes had submitted a claim, declaring that the building had been 'wantonly and maliciously blown up and destroyed' and that he would be seeking £100,000 in compensation. It was not long before the relevant authorities discovered that Weymes's statement had been something of an exaggeration. While the castle was unquestionably in a poor condition, this was due to insufficient maintenance over several years, which had led to widespread water ingress. A brief official report noted that 'the roof, the floor and the windows were undamaged except for a considerable amount of glass broken. The walls, staircases undamaged.' The only part of the castle which had suffered from the attack was what was described as a 'sanitary annexe', which had been gutted by fire, and seven panelled oak doors. Unable to dispose of the property, for which he had taken out a mortgage, it appears Weymes hoped to improve his financial circumstances by lodging an inflated claim. If this were the case, his efforts proved unsuccessful and when compensation was agreed, it was for just £1000.

Weymes never saw the money because, soon after making his claim, he was declared bankrupt: the compensation went back to the state, since he owed over £2000 to Revenue. By September 1923 his home and its contents were offered at auction, and the following March the family business premises were also on the market. Weymes moved to the United States where he found employment in various capacities until returning back to Westmeath in 1932: he died in 1969 at the age of ninety. As for Clonyn Castle, thereafter it went through various incarnations, being occupied for a time by a group of Australian nuns who tried, without success, to establish a school on the premises, after which another religious order used the place as a junior noviciate. In the second half of the 1940s a wealthy Mancunian, Yankel Levy, bought the castle and grounds so that it could be used as a centre for Jewish refugee children rescued from German concentration camps. Today it is once more a private home.

8

'This was the end of this home of my fathers'
BESSBOROUGH, COUNTY KILKENNY

IN 1784 ENGLISH artist Thomas Rowlandson produced one of his most celebrated watercolours. Subsequently issued as a popular print, the work depicts a scene in what was then London's fashionable place of public entertainment, Vauxhall Gardens. Like a photograph from a celebrity magazine, the picture is crowded with famous figures, among them the Prince of Wales with his former mistress Mrs Robinson on one side, lexicographer Dr Johnson and his amanuensis James Boswell on the other. But occupying centre stage and dominating the prospect are two women sauntering along arm in arm, seemingly oblivious of the attention they have attracted from an attendant crowd. These were the two sisters Georgiana, Duchess of Devonshire and Henrietta, Viscountess Duncannon, leaders of late-eighteenth-century aristocratic society.

The joys and travails of Georgiana Devonshire are well known, not least her unhappy marriage and excessive fondness of gambling. Her sibling, however, is less well remembered, despite being just as beautiful, wilful and extravagant, and leading a life just as crowded with incident. Georgiana, the elder, had married William, fifth Duke of Devonshire just as she turned seventeen. Henrietta, or Harriet as she was always known, was two years older when she in turn married Frederick Ponsonby, Viscount Duncannon, only son and heir to the second Earl of Bessborough. The marriage was often stormy, in part due to both of them being irredeemable gamblers, which led to unpaid debts and thence to violent rows. Lord Duncannon was also given to outbursts of jealousy and inclined on occasion to abuse his wife in public. However, he had good reason to be jealous, since Harriet Duncannon sought comfort from spousal ill-treatment in a succession of affairs; she once remarked 'I can never love anyone just *a little*.' Nor was she necessarily discreet: Lord Byron, who in due course had a brief but famously passionate dalliance with Harriet's daughter, Lady Caroline Lamb, once described his erstwhile lover's mother as 'the hack whore of the last half century'. Harriet experienced a particularly intense relationship with playwright Richard Brinsley Sheridan, which led her husband to threaten divorce (he was persuaded against doing so by his brother-in-law, the Duke of Devonshire, who had his own marital complications). However, her most significant and long-lasting affair began in the mid-1790s, by which time she had become Countess of Bessborough. Her lover was a handsome, ambitious politician Granville Leveson-Gower, twelve years her junior, by whom she had two children. Then in 1809 and aged forty-eight, she recognized, like the Marschallin in Strauss's *Der Rosenkavalier*, that the time had come to release the younger man from her embrace so that he could marry. In this instance his bride was Lady Bessborough's own niece, likewise called Harriet, a daughter of her beloved sister, the Duchess of Devonshire.

Regardless of their marital and financial troubles, during the late eighteenth and early nineteenth centuries, the Bessboroughs were a significant presence in English society, invited to the most fashionable gatherings and even staying in the Prince Regent's fanciful pavilion in Brighton. In consequence, they must be categorized as members of that rightly deprecated caste: the absentee landlord. Yet looking at the Ponsonbys' earlier history, this ought not to have been the case. The first of the family to settle in Ireland had been Sir John Ponsonby, originally from Cumberland and colonel of a regiment of horse in the service of Oliver Cromwell. The latter appointed Sir John a commissioner for taking the depositions of Protestants concerning murders said to have been committed during the Confederate Wars. As a reward for his labours, he was granted a large parcel of forfeited land at Kildalton, County Kilkenny. It was said that Cromwell accompanied him to his new property and, on arriving there cried out 'Behold the land flowing with milk and honey which the Lord hath delivered into my hands.' Whether the story is true or not, the lands given to the Ponsonbys proved to be of excellent quality, thereby ensuring them a substantial income (even if this was never enough for the third Earl of Bessborough and his extravagant wife). Appointed sheriff of counties Wicklow and Kilkenny in 1654, and elected to represent the latter in the first post-Restoration Irish parliament, Sir John Ponsonby married as his second wife the heiress Elizabeth Folliott, in whose honour he renamed his new Irish estate Bessborough.

Sir John was succeeded in turn by his two sons, the first, Henry Ponsonby, dying without a son, the second, William Ponsonby and his wife, making up for this by having several boys as well as six daughters. Having spent many years in the Irish House of Commons, in due course William also managed to be elevated to the House of Lords, created Baron Bessborough in 1721 and Viscount Duncannon two years later. The next generation continued this ascent. Until then the Ponsonbys had wielded some influence in their immediate locale but were of little consequence on the national stage. Politically and socially ambitious, Brabazon Ponsonby, who inherited estate and title in 1724, set out to change this situation. He was helped by successive marriages to heiresses, the first of whom, Sarah Colvill (*née* Margetson) was already a widow and seemingly did not wish to wed again. She was persuaded to do so by a ruse worthy of a Mozart opera. Ponsonby, having persuaded the widow's maid to admit him to her Dublin townhouse early one morning, duly appeared at a window dressed only in a nightshirt, thereby giving the impression a wedding had already taken place. Furthermore, 'the city band who had been apprised of a wedding (the custom being to serenade newly married couples), shortly made their appearance, accompanied with the clamour of beggars, to congratulate the supposed bride and bridegroom on their happy nuptials'. The widow Colvill gracefully gave way, presumably to salvage what remained of her reputation. As a result, her new husband could now add to his existing property portfolio Bishopscourt, an estate in County Kildare producing an annual income of £1800.

Like the two previous generations, Lord Duncannon had sat in the House of Commons until moving on his father's death to the House of Lords. He would then acquire a sequence of other high offices, many of which further enhanced his prestige and his revenue stream alike, among them Privy Counsellor, Commissioner of the Revenue, Marshal of the Admiralty in Ireland and Lord Justice in Ireland. In 1739 his status was further improved when he became first Earl of Bessborough.

Some five years later, no doubt feeling the need for a residence more in keeping with his improved social status, he pulled down the country house erected by his grandfather and replaced it with another. The new Bessborough consisted of a main block 100 feet long and 80 feet deep with a facade of nine bays and two storeys over raised basement, the entrance reached by flights of steps: curved quadrants linked it to two-storey wings on either side. Although it is known that Sir Edward Lovett Pearce wrote a memorial about the house's setting some time before his death in 1733, the new Bessborough House's design is usually attributed to Francis Bindon, a gentleman architect from County Clare, also notable as a portraitist (he painted no less than four likenesses of his friend Dean Swift). Bindon was related by marriage to Pearce and collaborated with Richard Castle on several projects, so his credentials are sound. Nevertheless, it cannot be claimed Bessborough was one of his better works, and tellingly when George Stone, Archbishop of Armagh, visited the property in 1753 he confined himself to remarking that 'everything was perfectly right and extremely agreeable'. Other commentators were less kind. Writing in *The Beauties of Ireland* (1825) John Norris Brewer pertinently observed:

> The mansion of Bessborough is a spacious structure of square proportions, composed of hewn stone, but the efforts of the architect were directed to amplitude, and convenience of internal arrangement, rather than to beauty of exterior aspect ... Viewed as an architectural object, its prevailing characteristic is that of massy respectability.

Likewise in an essay on Bindon published in the *Irish Georgian Society Bulletin* in 1967, the Knight of Glin described Bessborough House's garden front as 'an uninspiring six-bay breakfront composition with a pair of Venetian windows clumsily adrift on the first floor'. Clearly struggling to find something to commend, the Knight observed: 'The redeeming architectural feature of the house is to be found in the fine handling of the shallow quadrants leading to the flanking pavilions ... The facing sides of the pavilions have niches and surmounting lunettes.' On the other hand, no one could deny the beauty of the house's surroundings, Thomas Creevey writing in 1828, 'This is a charming place. I ought to say, as to its position and surrounding scenery – magnificent.'

In *Views of the seats of Noblemen and Gentlemen in England, Wales, Scotland, and Ireland* (published 1823), J.P. Neale has left a description of the house's interior and some of its contents, both more impressive than the exterior. 'The Hall is large, handsome, and in some respects unique,' Neale informed his readers,

> for it is adorned by four Ionic columns of Kilkenny marble, each of the shafts consisting of one entire mass, 10 feet 6 inches high. The Saloon and Dining Room are furnished with several fine Pictures, deserving the attention of the connoisseur; particularly a Night

Piece; Peter's Denial, by Gerard Segers, formerly belonging to Monsieur De Piles; a Nativity, by J. Jordaens; three fine old copies after Corregio; Birds, by Hondekoeter; Dead Game and Fruit, by F. Snyders and De Bos; with several Landscapes by Lucatelli and Horizonti. In the Corridor, leading to the principal staircase, are placed two horns of the moose deer, remaining fast to the skull: they were found at the farm of Belline, in November, 1781, and are supposed to be the largest ever discovered; the length of each horn, from the extremity to the tip, is 6 feet 1 inch.

No doubt the recently created Earl of Bessborough expected the next generation to settle in the family's smart new residence and to become equally significant figures in Irish political life. His younger son, John Ponsonby, assuredly lived up to his parental ambitions, eventually securing perhaps the most important political position in the country: Speaker of the House of Commons. However, Lord Bessborough, would be disappointed by the behaviour of his elder son: in 1736 – by which time he was aged thirty-two and supposedly acting as Member of Parliament for the constituency of Kilkenny – William Ponsonby embarked on a Grand Tour of Europe. He would not return for two years, six months of which were spent on a voyage to Greece and Constantinople in the company of John Montagu, fourth Earl of Sandwich and the Swiss-born artist Jean-Étienne Liotard. When he finally came back to Ireland, it was only for a short time, just long enough to get married in July 1739. In his father's eyes the choice of bride must have appeared highly advantageous, because Lady Caroline Cavendish was eldest daughter of the third Duke of Devonshire, then Lord Lieutenant of Ireland. And thanks to this connection, William was soon appointed Chief Secretary for Ireland. Even better, four years later, his ambitious younger brother John married Lady Caroline's younger sister Elizabeth Cavendish, thereby firmly cementing links between the two families. Old Lord Bessborough could not have wished for better but his hopes were soon thwarted because by 1742 William and Caroline Ponsonby had effectively abandoned Ireland. She, it seems, did not care for her husband's native country and he, after all he had seen and experienced on his Grand Tour, appears to have found the place somewhat provincial. Furthermore, although he would sit in the Westminster Parliament (his father having taken care to secure an English, as well as an Irish peerage) and was appointed to various posts including Lord Commissioner of the Treasury and Postmaster General of Great Britain, William Ponsonby, unlike his father and brother, was never a political animal. Indeed, after resigning the Postmaster Generalship in 1766, he held no further public office until his death twenty-seven years later. Throughout that long period, the only time he sought to become actively involved in state affairs was in 1773 when the Irish parliament proposed taxing landlords absent from their estates for more than six months per year at a rate of two shillings in the pound on their property in Ireland. William Ponsonby was, for obvious reasons, opposed to the measure and played a leading role in ensuring the necessary legislation failed to pass.

The interests of the second Earl of Bessborough, as he became following his father's death in 1758 (caused, it appears, by the old man swallowing cherry stones), were primarily cultural and social. He was an early member of the Society of Dilettanti, founded in the mid-1730s and described a few years later by Horace Walpole as being '... a club, for which the nominal qualification is having been in Italy, and the real one, being drunk'. He was also a founder member of the Divan Club, another rather louche – and short-lived – body, with entry confined to those who had visited the Ottoman Empire. Some years before its establishment, the earl had been painted in full Turkish garb by Jean-Étienne Liotard, first encountered on that voyage to Greece and Constantinople: a portrait of his wife in similar attire was also commissioned. Lord Bessborough would be Liotard's most important patron, eventually owning seventy-two of the artist's pictures. He was also an enthusiastic early supporter of Josiah Wedgwood, who wrote that the earl 'says he sees we shall exceed the Antients, that friezes & many other things may be made, that I am a very ingenious man ... & that he will do me every service in his power'. Lord Bessborough acquired a substantial collection of classical statuary (sold within a decade of his death by the heavily indebted next generation). Some of this he displayed in his London residence, a house in London's Cavendish Square. where he was rumoured to have had an affair with one of his neighbours, Princess Amelia, an unmarried daughter of George II. The rumour seems improbable: once when she came to dine with him, he clasped her hands so warmly that she exclaimed, 'My Lord, you are very good, but I wish you would not paw me so.' According to Lady Mary Coke, the earl, some time after becoming widowed, also proposed marriage to the princess, in response to which she 'laughed to such a degree that she could hardly stand'. Despite which, the two remained friends, Princess Amelia appointing him one of the executors of her will and leaving him £1000 in stock.

At Roehampton on the outskirts of London and overlooking Richmond Park, Lord Bessborough commissioned a neoclassical villa designed around 1760 by Sir William Chambers. The villa remained in the possession of the family until the middle of the nineteenth century when sold by the fifth earl, after which it became a Jesuit novitiate (where poet Gerald Manley Hopkins spent a couple of years); today it is part of the University of Roehampton. An anonymous poem, *On the Earl of Bessborough's Villa at Roehampton*, provides some sense of the building's character (and that of its original owner) in the years following its construction:

Here Genius Taste & Science stand confest
And fill the minds of each transposed Guest ...
Wheree'r (sic) we turn, where'er we look around
We seem to breathe & tread on Classic Ground ...
Ask ye, from whence these various Treasures came
These Scenes of Wonder? Need I Bessborough name?

During this period, back in Ireland Bessborough, the splendid residence erected only a few decades earlier and intended by the first earl to be the principal family seat, stood unoccupied. It would remain so for many years to come. Even after his father's death in July 1758 – and that of his wife a mere eighteen months later – the second earl does not appear to have spent any time in the house, although the drawing room was notable for a white marble chimney piece, which had carved female figures on either side, these supposedly representing Catherine, Duchess of St Albans and Charlotte, Countess Fitzwilliam: the two women were Lord Bessborough's daughters. Yet despite his absence, the building was never allowed to fall into disrepair. In October 1785 the first Earl of Portarlington and his wife visited the estate, and she wrote afterwards to her sister that it was 'a charming place with very fine old timber, and a very good house with some charming pictures, and it felt as warm and comfortable as if the family had left it the day before, and it has not been inhabited these forty years, which I think does great credit to the maid who has care of it'.

These circumstances scarcely changed in the aftermath of the second earl's death in 1793. His son and heir Frederick, husband of the beautiful Harriet Spencer, appears not even to have visited Ireland until he inherited the estate whence derived both his title and income. In July 1793 he arrived at Bessborough for the first time and, like the Portarlingtons before him, found all in good order. 'I came here yesterday,' he informed his wife,

> and am indeed very much pleased with the place. You and several people might have come and found everything ready; it really has answered my expectations ... The house is large & very comfortable, but as you may suppose, very old fashioned. There are about 10 or 11 good bedchambers. You would make it very cheerful with cutting down the windows, & I believe I should agree. There are several good pictures about the house. I have just discovered a Claude Lorrain. Soon after I arrived, I was saluted by

the peasants who came to dance in the court. We reckoned about 500 men & women, we gave them 2 barrels of beer & they seemed well pleased.'

So little was he familiar with his inheritance that the new Lord Bessborough expressed constant surprise at what he found: 'The mountains are beautiful over fine wood, & the verdure is the finest that can be seen ... The extent of the estate about it is very great, there are twenty seven thousand English acres all lying together here belonging to me.' However, as though anticipating the threat of his wife running up fresh gambling debts, he warned that a good deal of the land was let on long leases '& you must not from that suppose me very rich'.

Despite his delight in the family estate, Lord Bessborough only stayed there for a few days before returning to England. No wonder when William Tighe published his *Statistical survey of the County of Kilkenny* in 1802, he noted, 'The principal absentee proprietor is the Earl of Bessborough, who possesses 17,000 acres in the county, about 2,000 of which are let forever ... Though not inhabited for forty years, the house is kept in excellent order.' It would not be until October 1808 that the third earl came back to Ireland, this time accompanied by his wife, the couple spending a week on the estate. Like her husband before her, Harriet Bessborough was thrilled with what she found, writing from the house to her lover Leveson-Gower, 'I like this place extremely; with a very little expense it might be made *magnificent*, and it is beautiful ...' Of course, for that to happen, she would have had to remain in Ireland, but the main purpose of the visit on this occasion appears to have been a journey west in order to tour the Lakes of Killarney, then developing a reputation as a fashionable destination. From Kerry she wrote again to Leveson-Gower, telling him how the boatmen lamented that the two local landlords, Lord Kenmare and Mr Herbert, had moved to England; 'they make the most of Estates they never see; the trees are all to be cut down for timber, and the money sent to them'. The similarities with her own situation seem not to have occurred to Lady Bessborough.

The couple's next visit was in August 1812, this time accompanied by their daughter Lady Caroline Lamb, who they had brought with them in the hope of ending her infatuation with Lord Byron. In this endeavour they were unsuccessful. Nor, despite once more declaring delight with what they found in Ireland, did they linger in the country and after the family's departure, their Irish home was once again left standing empty. No wonder, therefore, that when visiting Bessborough with its heir, the future fourth earl, in 1828, English politician and diarist Thomas Creevey should have written, that although the house had been built as a family residence by the first earl:

> His son left Ireland when 18 years old and having never seen it more, died in 1792. Upon that event his Son, the present Lord Bessborough, made his first visit to the place, and he is not certain whether it was *two* or *three* days he staid here, but it was one or the other. In 1808, he and Lady Bessborough came on a tour to the Lakes of Killarney and having taken their own house in their way either going or coming, they were so pleased with it as to stay here a week, and once more in 1812, having come over to see the young Duke of Devonshire at Lismore, when his Father died, they were here a month. So that from 1757 to 1825, 68 years, the family was (here) 5 weeks and two days … My dears, it is absenteeism on the part of landlords, and the havoc that middlemen make with their property, that plays the very devil.

It is hard not to agree with Creevey's assessment. Nevertheless, the house continued to be perfectly maintained and, according to Brewer, writing in 1825, filled with treasures: he wrote that Bessborough House contained a 'valuable collection of pictures' including 'some excellent specimens of the Italian and Flemish schools' not least the Claude Lorrain already spotted by the third earl thirty years earlier.

In addition, Brewer noted hanging on the walls work by the likes of Titian, Domenichino, Raphael, Veronese, Rubens, Rembrandt, Van Dyck, Holbein, Guido Reni, Caracci, Maratta and Jordaens. Even allowing for some questionable attributions, this is an impressive list.

Circumstances finally changed with the arrival of the next generation. In 1826, a year after Brewer had visited the property, the fourth earl, then still going by the courtesy title of Lord Duncannon, came to Ireland with his wife and eleven children (there would eventually be fourteen). Since 1805 Duncannon had sat in the House of Commons representing English seats. Now he contested Kilkenny and won, with the result that – astonishingly, considering his grandfather's and father's lack of engagement with their estate – he chose to remain living in the country until his death twenty-one years later: the year before this occurred, he was appointed Lord Lieutenant of Ireland, the first resident landlord to hold that office since the Act of Union. It is easy to understand why he was offered the position. Despite not being an especially eloquent public speaker, the fourth earl, as he became on his father's death in 1844, was much admired. 'He had a remarkably calm and unruffled temper, and very good sound sense,' wrote the perceptive diarist Charles Greville. 'The consequence was that he was consulted by everybody, and usually and constantly employed in the arrangement of difficulties, the adjustment of rival pretensions, and the reconciliation of differences.'

Thanks to Creevey's letters to his stepdaughter Elizabeth Ord, more is known about the Bessborough estate at this time than had been the case earlier. Of the fourth earl's wife, Creevey observed:

> Her life here is devoted to looking after everybody, and in making them clean and comfortable in their persons, cloaths, cottages and everything ... I wish you could have seen us walking up Piltown [the local village] last Saturday. Good old Irish usage ... is to place the dirt and filth of the house at the entrance instead of behind it, and this was reformed at every house but one as we walked

thro' and Duncannon having called the old woman out told her he would not have the filth remain in that place ... to which she was pleased to reply, 'Well, my dear, if you do but walk by next Tuesday not a bit of the dirt shall you see remaining.'

The suspicion arises that the Duncannons were inclined to act as benign despots, ruling over their tenants with iron fist inside snugly fitting velvet glove. Creevey reported:

> My Lady's mode of travelling is on a little pony, she sitting sideways in a chair saddle; one of the little girls was on another pony. My Lord and I sauntered on foot by her side. She got off and went into different cottages as we went. She gives prizes for the cleanest cottages ... She put her Cottagers in mind of it, but there is a simplicity and interest and kindness in every communication of hers with the people here, on their part a natural unreserved confidential kind of return ...

No doubt worn out by her endeavours to improve the lives of her husband's tenants, Lady Duncannon died in 1834 at the age of forty-six. Her husband followed her thirteen years later, after which three of the couple's seven sons became successively Earls of Bessborough. The fifth holder of that title did not enjoy the same political success as his father, acting for some sixteen years as Master of the Buckhounds, an office in the royal household. His first wife Lady Frances Lambton died of consumption just sixteen weeks after the couple married, and it was not until fourteen years later that he ventured to remarry. This union soon also suffered setbacks: on their honeymoon, his bride Lady Caroline Gordon-Lennox accidentally blinded her new husband in one eye with her parasol: the lasting effect, it appears, was to leave him 'rather sharp-tempered'.

Neither union produced children, so when the fifth earl died in 1880, he was succeeded by the next-eldest brother, Frederick Ponsonby, a barrister whose main interests hitherto had been cricket and amateur theatricals. However, soon after becoming Earl of Bessborough he was asked by the British government to chair a commission examining earlier Landlord and Tenant Acts, with a view to improving relations between these two parties. The commission's conclusion – that 'Freedom of contract, in the case of the majority of Irish tenants, large and small, does not really exist' would lead to the Land Law Act of 1881, which for the first time gave tenants security of tenure.

The sixth earl never married, and on his death in 1895 the Bessborough estate and title passed once more down to the line to the next brother, Walter Ponsonby, an Anglican clergyman who had until then been acting as rector in a succession of English parishes. He was, however, married and with his wife Lady Louisa Eliot had eight children. The great house in County Kilkenny once more became a family home, evidence of which was apparent in structural work undertaken on the building. Until then it had risen two storeys above a half-exposed rusticated basement, with the pedimented first floor entrance reached via a double staircase. Now the area immediately in front of the central block was lowered, leaving the basement fully exposed as a new ground floor centred on a substantial porte-cochère providing access to the interior. Here a new entrance hall was created, while its predecessor above was turned into a sitting room. This work was undertaken by architect Sir Thomas Manly Deane.

When the clerical seventh earl died in 1906, the Bessborough title and lands were inherited by his eldest son Edward Ponsonby, a qualified barrister and businessman who served on a number of company boards, such as that of Gordon Hotels (judged at the start of the twentieth century as the largest such group in the world) and the London, Brighton and South Coast Railway, of which he acted as chairman for many years: all very different from the indolence exhibited by his antecedents a century earlier. The eighth earl's various obligations meant he could not live in Ireland all the time, but the family regularly came to stay at Bessborough House, where they entertained large parties of friends for long periods. On one occasion, Queen Victoria's son the Duke of Connaught and his wife paid a visit, and were entertained with a concert at which one of the other houseguests, Marguerite Connellan, sang Percy French's ballad 'The Mountains of Mourne'; she was supposed to do so in her bare feet but forgot and instead wore bedroom slippers. During this period Bessborough was also notable for its amateur dramatic performances, a popular pastime in the Edwardian era; Vere Ponsonby, future ninth Earl of Bessborough was a keen actor and even brought over a professional director from London when *The Merchant of Venice* was staged in the house.

Like his father, Vere, Lord Duncannon had qualified as a barrister but soon entered politics, becoming a member of London County Council in 1907 before being elected to the Westminster Parliament for the first time. Following his father's example, he also enjoyed a successful business career, acting as chairman of a number of major companies such as the Sao Paulo Railway, and deputy chairman of De Beers Consolidated Mines. Following the outbreak of the First World War, he joined the army and rose to the rank of acting major; his younger brother Myles was not so fortunate and was killed in September 1915 while on active service.

The ninth earl believed that his mother never fully recovered from the shock of losing one of her sons and indeed less than a year after peace was declared, she died in Ireland. The following September 1920, her widowed husband, then aged sixty-nine, was staying at Bessborough together with one of his sisters and a niece. In the early hours of the morning, the place was raided, the earl afterwards recording that some fifteen masked men wielding revolvers had turned up at the front door and demanded entry. When the door was eventually opened by the cook and housekeeper, the raiders declared they were in search of arms and ammunition in the name of the 'Irish Republic'. Earlier that year, Lord Bessborough had handed over all sporting guns to troops in Waterford, so there were none in the house but that did not deter the men, although when instructed by the housekeeper to take off their masks and put down their revolvers, they did so. Despite being told that the elderly owner was unwell and confined to bed with sciatica, the group's leaders insisted on being brought to his bedroom, where he told them again that there were no guns, rifles, revolvers or ammunition on the premises. Nevertheless, they demanded to be brought to the gunroom. Only after finding this empty did they return to the rest of the men – being kept in the hall by one of the servants – gathered their belongings, and left. Before doing so, one of the leaders rightly congratulated the maid, cook and housekeeper on their plucky behaviour. According to the earl, that same night the group 'had previously visited four or five farms outside the Park walls, where they got a gun at each, then two lodges of mine and the Steward's house – nothing taken – then the Agent's house, where they unfortunately took away his uniform'.

Writing some time later, Lord Bessborough's son Vere, the ninth earl, noted that the raiders had told his father that times had changed: 'I think that this personal experience of the change that had indeed come over Ireland broke his heart.' The eighth earl never returned to Bessborough. Three months later, at the beginning of December 1920 he travelled to Birmingham to attend a dinner held by the engineering company Guest, Keen & Nettlefolds, of which he was chairman. At the end of the meal he stood up and made a speech in which he told the rest of those present what had happened while he was in Ireland. He then sat down, had a heart attack, and died.

His heir, now ninth earl, had already been advised not to travel to Ireland, having sat in Parliament for some years as a unionist member. With the War of Independence at its height, none of the family visited Bessborough during 1921 and, aware that the building was at risk of attack, its owner took the precaution of having sent to London around a dozen of the best paintings and all the plate, 'on the plea that the pictures wanted cleaning & that we were short of plate, for any considerable signs of removal were regarded by the rebels as "provocative" & liable to attract their attention'. In January 1922, during a lull between the War of Independence and the Civil War, the earl and his French wife Roberte came to Ireland for ten days. 'At Bessborough,' he remembered, 'all seemed peaceful, on the surface, the only visible example of changed conditions being our seeing two men walking across the Park & past the House on Sunday afternoon with guns on their shoulders without attempt at concealment.'

The family then left, expecting to return again during the autumn. Their plans changed when, in August, a number of members of the anti-Treaty forces took over the servants' wing at Bessborough House for a fortnight. Already during the previous couple of months raids had seen various items such as mattresses, blankets, kitchen tables and chairs taken from the property. In addition, fruit and vegetables, butter and milk were stolen from the estate, a number of trees cut down, and a pony and trap commandeered for ten days. In July, in the nearby village of Fiddown, a former two-storey police barracks – which belonged to the Bessboroughs but had been seized by anti-Treaty forces – was burnt down (a claim was lodged for £1450; the eventual award, made in June 1927, was for £950, conditional on full reinstatement). Lord Bessborough understandably decided to remove a further twenty pictures from the main house and have them sent to London, together with a collection of miniatures and other small items. The following month, 'I got over to London the Chippendale tables from the dining room & a set of ten of the best of the Chippendale chairs, as well as six Jacobean chairs from the Canford Room.'

He was right to have taken what he could from the house because it was only a matter of time before the place would suffer serious attack. On 23 February 1923 two men wrote to the earl, one being a member of the estate staff, John Holland. 'I do feel so sorry to report that Bessborough House was burned last night,' he informed the building's owner. 'About 40 men broke in the front door about 11 o'c & sprayed the rooms with petrol & set them on fire.' Household staff did what they could to rescue some of the house's contents, saving a number of pieces of furniture and two busts, but much was lost, not least because the local fire engine broke down while on the way and by the time it finally arrived, the flames were too far gone. Fortunately, the servants' own quarters were spared destruction by the expedient of cutting the roof between that part of the building and the main house. The second letter came from Piltown's parish priest, Canon Thomas Phelan, lamenting the destruction of Bessborough. 'Accept my very sincere sympathy,' he wrote, 'and in it, my curates and my parishioners join.' Evidently wishing to distance anyone in the area from responsibility for the fire, he explained:

> The district had resumed normality, but my fear, that the torchbearers who did so much damage in Waterford would cross the river, have proven to be well grounded. Alas! Alas! That a few can do so much harm. Thank God no life was lost, but it is maddening that such valuable property can be destroyed with impunity.

A compensation claim was soon submitted by the Bessboroughs' agent, Major Max Bollam. The sum requested was £100,000 but this figure was later revised to £51,422 for the house and its reconstruction, and £16,744 for the loss of contents. As so often, it took some time to process the claim and various intercessions were made to figures of authority in the hope that these might encourage greater speed. In November 1924 Canon Phelan wrote to the president asking that the Bessborough case might be settled as soon as possible. 'Owing to the great want of employment,' he explained, 'the people would be very grateful if you could accelerate the hearing of the claim.' Not only would the rebuilding of the house provide work locally, but its destruction had left many former staff without jobs: 'The coachman, two grooms, four housemaids, a painter, a plasterer, a mason and some 10 or 12 others.' The priest's letter received a typically courteous but non-committal response from the president's office.

By then John Butler, an employee of the Office of Public Works, had been despatched to County Kilkenny to investigate the validity of the Bessboroughs' claim for loss of contents. Having interviewed the housekeeper, Mrs O'Keeffe, and a number of other persons, he duly reduced the value of what had been destroyed to £13,116 (the eventual sum awarded was £13,700). Butler's colleague in the same organization, Thomas Martin, likewise examined the claim for compensation and assistance in rebuilding the house and was even more ruthless in cutting down the figure requested. His report, submitted in December 1924, proposed removing £3553 from the amount sought on the grounds that this figure represented a 'saving to the claimant in upkeep, which will follow the substitution of a practically new building for one 200 to 250 years old'. Martin reckoned the cost of rebuilding the house amounted to no more than £20,300. He argued, for example, that there was no need to take down the entire parapet wall and balustrade of the house, but only to replace damaged sections. He also proposed that the dismantling and reconstruction of chimney shafts was unnecessary as they were in good condition, and 'any dilapidations they show are on account of exposure to the elements and are not due to damage by the recent fire'. It does not seem to have occurred to him that, but for the fire, the shafts would never have been exposed to the elements.

Major Bollam, the Bessborough agent, was quick to spurn Martin's revised sums, informing the relevant officials in the Office of Public Works that he stood by the figures in the claim 'which were, he says, prepared by well-paid experts and he does not see why he should accept less than those figures until the experts advise him to do so'. Negotiations continued until mid-May 1925 when a sum of £32,000 was agreed, on condition the house be rebuilt. When redress was added for the loss of furniture and other contents, the total came to £45,700, plus costs of just over £760. Of this, £34,760 was to be paid in cash and £11,700 in securities, but all of it dependent on receipt of bills proving reconstruction work had taken place.

The earl asked an old friend from his days at Cambridge University, architect Harry Stuart Goodhart-Rendel, to oversee the restoration work at Bessborough. Goodhart-Rendel had stayed in the house on several occasions before the First World War and, in an article published in *Country Life* in 1982, architectural writer Clive Aslet quoted his observation that when it came to reconstructing the building, his client 'relied on my memory for the character of what new internal detail we were able to put in'. In fact, it does not appear that the house benefitted much from internal detail since the rooms were left undecorated, the only distinctive space being a double-height entrance hall with a polished marble staircase that runs up to a screened and vaulted passageway with balustraded gallery on the opposite wall.

The Free State government's twenty-seventh and final payment for the rebuilding of Bessborough was made in mid-July 1930, more than seven years after the fire. A report in the *Irish Independent* after the compensation award had been agreed in May 1925 noted with delight that the family intended to return to Ireland and taken up residency in their old home. This never happened. A year after the house had been burnt, the Bessboroughs had bought Stansted Park, a large Edwardian property at the centre of an 1800-acre estate in West Sussex and had commissioned Harry Goodhart-Rendel to carry out alterations. This now became the family's home, furnished with furniture and pictures sensibly removed from Bessborough prior to the fire. In early 1931 the earl was appointed Governor General of Canada, a position he held until November 1935, meaning he lived on the other side of the Atlantic for the next four years. Bessborough, although restored, once more stood empty, as it had during the second half of the eighteenth century. By the end of the 1930s the family had entirely disposed of their County Kilkenny estate. Soon afterwards the house and demesne were bought by a religious order, the Oblate Fathers, who established a seminary on the site, adding large and resolutely workaday wings on either side of the building; the architect of these extensions, if one was ever employed, is deservedly unknown. In 1971 the estate was bought by the Irish Department of Agriculture and ever since has operated as a state-run agricultural college. Its name changed back to Kildalton, all ties with the Ponsonby family have been decisively severed.

9

'All gone, all scattered and we were so happy there'
DESART COURT, COUNTY KILKENNY

AT THE VERY END of the nineteenth century, Captain the Hon. Otway Cuffe settled in County Kilkenny, close to an estate held by his family for the previous 250 years. Although he had previously served in the British army and as aide-de-camp to the Duke of Connaught, was Groom of the Privy Chamber to Queen Victoria (and Gentleman Usher to her son Edward VII), the captain now became a fervent supporter of the Gaelic Revival, expressed among other ways in his choice of clothing. He took to wearing what he believed to be correct Irish dress and while eschewing the saffron kilt favoured by some fervent nationalists at the time, clad himself in dark blue, full-skirted coat, breeches and stockings, and flat shoes, his head covered with a wide, soft hat. As remembered by one of his nieces, who knew him as Uncle Dot, 'it was a good costume and well suited to his tall robust figure. But no one save himself ever knew why he thought it an Irish dress.'

What might the captain's forebears, the Cuffes who originally settled in Ireland, have made of their descendant's charming eccentricities? When the first of them arrived in the country in the sixteenth century, the adoption of local dress would have been far from his thoughts, unless perhaps for the purpose of tricking the native population. It was another captain, John Cuffe from Somerset, who originally came to Ireland in 1561 but just three years later he was dead, having been fatally wounded during a skirmish in County Wexford. This unfortunate end seems not to have deterred other members of the family, because in 1587 Captain John's nephew, Hugh Cuffe, was to be found in County Cork where he had been granted land by Elizabeth I, part of the English Crown's division of the vast lands hitherto held by the FitzGerald earls of Desmond. Meanwhile Hugh Cuffe's brother Henry served as private secretary to Robert Devereux, Earl of Essex, accompanying him on his ill-fated expedition to Ireland in 1599 (two years later, he also shared the earl's fate when the latter fell from royal favour, and was executed ten days after his erstwhile master). Hugh Cuffe also suffered a few setbacks because he was forced to hand back at least some of the land granted to him in County Cork after his right to it had been challenged by members of an Old English family related to the FitzGeralds. Nevertheless, he must have held onto some of it because a marriage settlement drawn up in 1604 between his daughter Dorothea and Charles Coote, describes Hugh Cuffe as being 'of Cuffe's Wood (or Kilmore), County Cork'. Coote, an English adventurer like his father-in-law, was evidently so enchanted by his bride that when he embarked on building a fine new residence in County Laois in 1621, named the place Castle Cuffe. Neither the house nor its begetter ultimately fared well: Coote was shot dead in 1642 while leading a cavalry charge against an Irish Confederate army in Trim, County Meath, and around the same time Castle Cuffe was attacked and burned by the O'Dunnes, former owners of the land on which it stood.

Although faced with similar challenges, another branch of the Cuffe family enjoyed better fortune. Maurice Cuffe is thought to have been a merchant in Ennis, County Clare, where his son Joseph was born, probably around 1621. Having served as a cavalryman in Oliver Cromwell's Commonwealth army, Joseph Cuffe duly benefitted from its victory when he was awarded lands at Castleinch, just a few miles outside Kilkenny city: these had previously been held by the St Leger and Comerford families. Joseph's ownership of this property was duly

confirmed following the restoration of Charles II, a document dated
October 1666 referring 1200 acres 'to be called and known for ever by
the name of Cuffe's Desart'. Twelve years earlier, already sufficiently
secure in his ownership of the property, Joseph Cuffe had married
Martha Muschamp, whose father was another soldier of English
origin, the splendidly titled Colonel Agmondesham Muschamp. His
memory would be perpetuated by successive generations of Cuffes
who were given the same first name.

The earliest of them was Joseph and Martha's eldest son and heir
(they had twenty children in total, although not all survived into
adulthood), Agmondesham Cuffe. In 1678, a year before his father's
death, he married the widowed Anne Warden whose great-grandson
(from her previous marriage) was the late-eighteenth-century Irish
statesman Henry Flood. Anne Warden's father, Sir John Otway, was
a member of the Westminster House of Commons and served as
a member of the Privy Council during the first years of James II's
reign. His son-in-law was less favourably inclined towards the king,
an attitude clearly reciprocated because in December 1687 a royal
charter called for the dismissal of Agmondesham Cuffe from both
Kilkenny Corporation and the office of Mayor of Kilkenny, to which
he had only been elected six months before. His continued enjoyment
of the lands at Castleinch granted to his father was also threatened.
It is therefore hardly surprising that Cuffe chose to back William III,
ensuring that when the latter confirmed his authority in Ireland after
the Battle of the Boyne, he also confirmed his supporter's rights to the
estate. In 1695 Cuffe was elected, under questionable circumstances,
to represent County Kilkenny in the Irish House of Commons: a
subsequent enquiry showed that he had illegally created a large
number of freeholders so that they would vote for him.

Agmondesham Cuffe's character appears in contrast to that of
his son and heir John, later described by one of his descendants,
Dorothea Herbert, as 'a remarkably handsome and good man'. Like
his father he secured a seat in the House of Commons, representing

Thomastown, although in this instance there were no accusations of vote rigging; indeed, within a few years he was awarded an honorary doctorate by his alma mater Trinity College Dublin for services rendered in Parliament. His first wife Margaret Hamilton appears not to have lived long, and in 1726 he married a second time, his bride being Dorothea Gorges. Her parents' marriage had not been happy and the couple had parted within a few years of their daughter's birth, owing to what was described as her father Colonel Richard Gorge's 'abandoned and dissolute conduct'.

Dorothea's mother, Nicola Sophia Hamilton – who had suffered from that conduct and hence initiated the separation – was the principal figure in one of Ireland's most famous ghost stories, known as The Black Velvet Ribbon. Orphaned young, she had been brought up with her cousin John de la Poer, second Earl of Tyrone. As teenagers, they took a vow that whichever of them died first would return to the other to tell of what took place in the afterlife. In due course Nicola Hamilton married Sir Tristram Beresford and one morning in October 1693, while staying at Gill Hall, County Down, she appeared at breakfast with a wide band of black velvet ribbon around the wrist of her left hand. She refused to explain why she wore this, but said that she would never be seen in company again without it. Before breakfast ended, a servant appeared with a letter edged in black: 'It is as I expected,' Lady Beresford remarked, 'Lord Tyrone is dead.'

What was the explanation for the ribbon, and for the premonition of her cousin's death? The previous night, while she was in bed, Lord Tyrone had suddenly appeared before her and when she asked why he was there, he reminded her of the pact they had made many years before. He was dead, but had returned 'to assure you that revealed religion is the only true one'. He then told her that she would in due course give birth to a son who would marry his daughter, that her husband would subsequently die and she would marry a second time, to a man who would make her very unhappy. Finally, he warned her that she would then die at the age of forty-seven. Doubting the veracity of what he had said, Lady Beresford asked for proof that it was true. He lifted her bedcurtains, but she said this might all be a dream. He laid two fingers on an adjacent piece of furniture and left a mark but she said this could be an overnight accident. He wrote a few words in a notebook but this she said she might have done herself. Finally, he told her to stretch out her arm and touched her wrist. 'His hand was as cold as marble,' she later reported, and instantly the sinews of her wrist shrank and every nerve withered. The apparition told her not to show anybody the mark, and then vanished. The following day, she appeared at breakfast with the ribbon around her left wrist.

In due course, all that her cousin had predicted came to pass. The next summer, her son Sir Marcus Beresford was born but within a few years her husband died and she made the unfortunate second marriage to Richard Gorges, father of John Cuffe's future wife Dorothea. Cuffe never met his mother-in-law because she died suddenly in 1713. The previous year, when she turned forty-seven, she had been filled with dread, given that everything else her cousin told her had come to pass. But as the months went by, and nothing happened, she began to believe the anticipated threat to her life would not be realized. Finally, on 23 February 1713, she decided to invite some friends to gather for a celebration of her forty-eighth birthday. Among the guests was an elderly clergyman who had baptized her and when she explained the reason for the party, he spoke up to say that she was mistaken about the year of her birth: she was now aged only forty-seven. 'You have pronounced my death warrant,' his hostess declared before retiring to her room where her son joined her and was told the whole story. She then lay down on her bed where, a few hours later, she was found dead.

John Cuffe seems to have been untroubled by the strange history of his wife's mother, but perhaps any scruples he may have entertained were overcome thanks to the £10,000-worth of silver plate which his wife brought to the marriage. According to his niece Dorothea Herbert, the plate had been 'taken by her father at the Siege of Quebec' although this seems unlikely since that event took place in 1759, by which time John Cuffe had been dead ten years.

Long before then, he and his wife had had nine children, of which seven lived beyond childhood. Perhaps because of this growing family, or perhaps due to the fact that in November 1733 he was elevated to the peerage as Baron Desart of Desart, John Cuffe now embarked on building a new residence for himself, abandoning the Castleinch tower house, which had provided a home for his forebears. Dorothea Herbert, whose mother Martha Cuffe grew up in what came to be called Desart Court, would write that, surrounded by fine woods and old oaks:

> The House is a very Grand one much like Bessborough but its chief Beauty is its two Superb Staircases and Noble Gallery – It is altogether a very grand and venerable place and I felt a pleasure in hearing my mother recount the Many Happy Hours she spent in the large Hall where in my Grandfather's time the family met and dined round a blazing Wood fire after the Manner of Old Times.

Much later, in 1915, Thomas Sadleir and Page Dickinson likewise enthused about the house, constructed of blue limestone and following the fashion for Palladianism in having a seven-bay, two-storey-over-basement central block with quadrants leading to pavilions on either side. Internal stylistic similarities with the former Archbishop's Palace in Cashel, County Tipperary, which was designed by Sir Edward Lovett Pearce, have long led to the belief that he was also responsible for Desart Court, which dates from the year of the renowned architect's death. Whether he had a hand here remains unproven but extant photographs show that Sadleir and Dickinson were right to be much taken with the rococo ceiling decoration in the main reception rooms, as well as the grand staircases found at either end of the main block. 'In no other case in Ireland,' they wrote, 'have we found the handsome carved scroll-work in oak, in lieu of balusters, such as we have here.'

The construction of such a large mansion was an expensive business, and must have consumed much of the £10,000 in plate that Dorothea Gorges had brought to the marriage. Nevertheless, further expenditure followed, not least the purchase in 1735 of another estate at Callan from the Earl of Arran for £11,120 (thirty years later in 1765, shortage of funds meant his heir would be obliged to sell some 2100 acres of this land, including the town of Callan, to another local man, James Agar). Having thus gone to the expense of setting himself up as a member of the landed aristocracy, in 1749 the new Lord Desart died in his new Desart Court.

The estate was inherited by his eldest son John, then aged nineteen and a student at Trinity College Dublin. It may have been during his time as an undergraduate that John Cuffe had an illegitimate son, Joseph Cuffe, who he acknowledged as his own child. The invaluable Dorothea Herbert recalled that this young man, having initially lived at Desart Court, came to stay with her own family (her father was a Church of Ireland rector in Carrick-on-Suir). She described her cousin Joseph as

> a mighty good Creature and much pleased with his new abode. I was then a very young child but a great pet of his and as he had a great taste for Music, drawings and the Belles Lettres, he strove to engraft a like taste on my Young Mind – he lent me all his books, gave me some chosen volumes and began to teach me to draw, but falling into a deep decay he left this and died soon after to the great grief of all the family who respected and loved him as much as if he had been Legitimated into it.

In 1752 Lord Desart married a widowed heiress, Sophia Badham, but the couple had only daughters before he died suddenly at the age of thirty-seven in November 1767. According to Dorothea Herbert, his demise was the result of catching a fever while he sat for his portrait, 'and what is more remarkable two Dogs and a fine Horse that were drawn in the Picture caught the Disorder – the Dogs died – the Horse was never any good after and the painter lost his sight – supposed from some poisonous paint'. A man 'universally beloved', she wrote that his funeral procession was some three miles long.

His brother Otway Cuffe had just turned thirty when he became third Lord Desart. As a younger son, he had not expected to inherit the estate and, after studying at Christ Church Oxford he had moved to London's Inner Temple and embarked on a legal career, although there is some indication that he also considered joining the army. All such plans were abandoned following his brother's death, as a result of which he became responsible for Desart Court. His niece Dorothea Herbert, while acknowledging that he was 'a good man', thought the new Lord Desart did not look after the family seat properly. He had, she wrote 'lived forty years a Bachelor and let the place go to wreck whilst he mostly resided in England'. The latter country had been his home since the age of fifteen, so it is not altogether surprising that he remained attached to it. But he did settle in Ireland, and served as Mayor of Kilkenny on a number of occasions, during which he introduced street lighting and rubbish collection to the city, as well as overseeing the reconstruction of the old Linen Market. These public services may explain why, in 1781, he was created Viscount Desart and twelve years later Earl of Desart. Between these two dates, in 1785 and at the age of forty-eight he finally married, his bride Lady Anne Browne being more than a quarter-century younger. A daughter of the second Earl of Altamont, her arrival improved the Cuffe family finances (Lady Anne's mother was Elizabeth Kelly, heiress to one of the greatest sugar plantations in Jamaica). The couple had three children, including a son, John Otway Cuffe, who was sixteen and a schoolboy at Eton College when his elderly father died in 1804. Unlike the latter, the second earl did not enjoy a long life, dying in 1820 at the age of thirty-two and leaving behind as his heir a two-year-old son, John Otway O'Connor Cuffe.

In 1842 the third earl married Lady Elizabeth Campbell, a daughter of the first Earl of Cawdor. They made an exceptionally good-looking couple: Benjamin Disraeli pronounced them 'the two most beautiful people I ever saw'. In 1848 the future Emperor Napoleon III paid a visit to Beaudesert Hall in Staffordshire at the same time as the Desarts and was asked what he thought of the place. '*J'aime beaucoup Beaudesert*,' he replied, '*mais encore plus la belle Desart.*'

Three years earlier Lady Desart had been appointed a Lady of the Bedchamber to Queen Victoria, occupying this position until 1864. In the meantime, she and her husband had a daughter and three sons, one of whom, the fifth earl, would recall their childhood in his charming, unfinished memoir *A Page from the Past*:

> For us children life at Desart was a permanent delight. The shrubberies and woods and park, the animals wild and domesticated, seemed to provide every pleasure that human nature could require. The centre of interest in the county of Kilkenny was fox-hunting. Old and young alike viewed it as of far greater importance than government, politics, or – I might even say – religion; and we children began our hunting career in perambulators, and continued on donkeys until we were promoted to the happiness of ponies. Horses and dogs, including the puppies we walked for the Kilkenny Hunt, became our bosom friends.

All that would change following the third earl's death at the relatively early age of forty-six. A sportsman, he never recovered from two bad falls, the first in the hunting field, the second on a yacht in Greece: left paralysed, he died in 1865.

The accidents that befell his father did not deter his eldest son, William Ulick O'Connor Cuffe, who throughout his life was a keen huntsman and yachtsman (he would die on board his own yacht). At the age of twenty, he now became fourth Earl of Desart but seems to have taken relatively little interest in his Irish estate, preferring to spend most of the time in England. In 1889 his aunt Maria La Touche visited Desart Court, which she had known as a child and sadly recorded, 'all the familiar walks were obliterated, the stones of the terraces and balustrades were lifted out of place by seedling trees ... there was something very sad about it from the human side. But yet I never saw the place look so beautiful or so stately and sad.' Lord Desart also had a literary bent, writing some thirteen novels. None of them now remain in print, and the fact that he published them with his name 'The Earl of Desart' suggests snobbery may have aided sales. Covering a variety of genres – mystery, science fiction, romance – the first of them, *Only a Woman's Love*, was published in 1869. Finding a woman's love for himself proved slightly more challenging for the fourth earl, perhaps because of his unprepossessing appearance: he was once described as 'one of the ugliest men in the United Kingdom', which is somewhat surprising given his parents' good looks. However, in 1871 he married Maria Preston, who unlike her husband was unquestionably attractive: Oscar Wilde called her 'the most lovely and dangerous woman in London'. The following year she gave birth to the couple's only child, a daughter called Kathleen. Thereafter the marriage began to unravel and in May 1878 Lord Desart sued his wife for divorce on the grounds of her adultery: the previous December he had discovered she was having an affair with another man. This was Charles Sugden, actor and sometime ringmaster, noted in an obituary as having been 'handsome, dashing, fascinating, an athlete of repute'. Letters read out in court during the Desart divorce proceedings indicated Sugden and the countess had been clandestinely meeting for some time, staying as a married couple in rented accommodation under assumed names. The proceedings were uncontested and a few months later Sugden and his lover were married in Paris (although this relationship also ended in divorce in 1891, seemingly when the former countess's money had run out).

In the meantime, her first husband had married again, his second wife being Ellen Odette Bischoffsheim, elder daughter and co-heiress of an exceedingly rich London banker: it was rumoured that she brought with her a dowry of £150,000 (with a similar sum due on her father's death). Curiously, the following year her sister Amelia also married an Irishman, Sir Maurice FitzGerald, Knight of Kerry. Unlike her predecessor, the new Countess of Desart and her husband, although they had no children, seem to have been extremely happy together: a stone over their joint tomb reads 'They were together in their lives, and in their deaths they shall not be divided.' He died suddenly in 1898, thirty-five years before she did, and although the couple had not spent so much time in Ireland, after his death she put forward a claim to the contents of Desart Court, and also proposed to her late husband's brother – who now became the fifth Earl of Desart – that she move into the house and live there, an offer he declined.

Nevertheless, the widowed Lady Desart opted to remain in the area, and became its most generous philanthropist, establishing a woollen mill, a basket factory and a tobacco farm, which ventures enjoyed varying degrees of success. Together with her other brother-in-law, the peculiarly costumed Captain the Hon. Otway Cuffe, she became a fervent supporter of the Gaelic League and after his death in 1912, took over as president of the local branch. Long before that she had paid for the establishment of a theatre in Kilkenny, as well as a dance hall, a handball court and recreation centre. In 1910, the year in which she was bestowed with the Freedom of the City, she supplied the site for a Carnegie Library, as well as its fittings, which were made by the Kilkenny Woodworkers, a firm established by Captain Cuffe but underwritten by her. The same company also made most of the furniture for Aut Even (from the Irish 'Áit Aoibhinn', meaning 'Beautiful Place'), an Arts and Crafts house she commissioned herself from architect William Scott on the outskirts of the city. Close by, she established the model village of Talbot's Inch and here also in 1915 the Aut Even Hospital. In the aftermath of the War of Independence, in December 1922 she was one of only four women appointed to the first Senate – ironically, some fifteen years earlier she had been a vocal opponent of women's suffrage – remaining in the position until her death in 1933.

Ellen Desart's passionate commitment to Ireland, and her support for projects that would improve the circumstances of the local population, makes the destruction of Desart Court all the more tragic, especially since its last owner, although not enjoying his sister-in-law's large income, similarly worked to do his best for the area.

Hamilton John Agmondesham Cuffe, fifth and final Earl of Desart, had not thought to inherit the estate. Indeed, as a younger son, his parents had made other plans for him: at the age of just twelve he was sent to live on board a vessel at Portsmouth while training to become a midshipman in the Royal Navy. A year later he sailed across the Atlantic in a leaky frigate called *Orlando*, part of force intended to protect British interests in the Caribbean following the onset of the American Civil War. It was two years before he returned home, by which time he had decided against a naval career and so, after sufficient schooling and then time at Cambridge University, thought to join the Foreign Office and become a diplomat. However, after failing the entrance exam, he had to think again and settled on the Bar as his best means of securing an adequate income. This had become essential because, by this time, he had fallen in love with his future wife, Lady Margaret Lascelles. She was one of the many children of the fourth Earl of Harewood, very grand, very aloof, who had so many offspring from his own two marriages that he scarcely knew some of them. It was said that on one occasion, walking in Hyde Park and seeing a nursery maid wheeling a pram with a couple of infants, he asked whose children they might be. 'Yours m'Lord' came the response.

However, he violently disapproved of the idea that his daughter Margaret, then barely out of the classroom and not yet presented to London society, should marry Hamilton Cuffe, younger son of a relatively impoverished Irish peer and a young man with few prospects. The couple were forbidden to meet and, for two years, not allowed even to correspond, although they did manage to exchange a few notes. Then, aside from a single encounter, although meetings continued to be proscribed, they were permitted to write. At the same time, all talk of marriage was not countenanced. Finally, after some six years, his legal career beginning to prosper and her personal circumstances improved thanks to a grandmother's legacy, permission was granted. The couple married in July 1876 and remained devoted to each other for the next half century. After her death in 1927 he wrote to their granddaughter Iris Origo, 'I believe that love in marriage is better than anything in life. Ambition and success are not in the running with it. My real life has always been my home – wife, children, grandchildren.'

Two years after the long-obstructed marriage, Hamilton Cuffe was invited to become Assistant Solicitor to the Treasury, and in due course would become Treasury Solicitor as well as Queen's Proctor and eventually Director of Public Prosecutions. Throughout much this time, although he might sometimes visit Desart Court at his older brother's invitation, it was not his home. Only with the fourth earl's sudden death in 1898 did it become so, allowing him to assume responsibility for a place he remembered so well from his happy childhood there. However, owing to his brother's widow being reluctant to relinquish a property she scarcely knew, a year had to pass before the fifth earl was actually able to take full possession of Desart Court. A week or so before he was able to visit, his wife and unmarried younger daughter Sybil travelled over from London to assess what needed to be done. 'The first view of Desart was entirely pleasing,' Lady Sybil Lubbock later remembered. 'Its admirable Italianate façade of Kilkenny marble, a fine dark limestone, looked both elegant and stately, and showed no signs of disrepair.' The main reception rooms likewise appeared to be in reasonable condition. The upper floors were another matter. 'It is a fact that a cupboard in one of the bedrooms contained not less than twenty-seven old and dilapidated high-hats, which will stand for the measure of the cleaning and tidying that had been attempted. The dust and litter of thirteen years lay everywhere almost undisturbed;

the task before us looked appalling.' Nothing had been done to modernize the house. Aside from what might be drawn from a well in the stable yard, for example, all water still had to be brought up from a stream below the park. Outside, the grounds had similarly been neglected, the walled garden, which should have been the source of fresh vegetables and fruit, shoulder-high in weed. But even by the time the new Lord Desart finally arrived, 'he could look over a terrace and park and woodland that were lovely and brilliant in the morning. He said nothing, and his look kept us silent too. Then he gave a sigh, it might have been of contentment, it might have been of memory. "I'm glad to be home," he said, and turned to my mother. But she had gone in to make the tea.'

Home it may have been, but the necessity of earning an income to support Desart Court, and to rescue it from the desuetude into which the estate had fallen, meant its owner had to continue working in London, visiting Ireland as often as he was able to do so. He would only leave his position in the Treasury in 1909. The income from his work allowed improvements to be carried out at Desart Court, both indoors and outside, although in the aftermath of the 1903 Wyndham Act the greater part of the estate was sold to tenants, with the family retaining just the demesne. Although the house was usually advertised to rent during the hunting season, when it was not taken the Desarts would often ride out with the hounds, Sybil Lubbock recalling 'a cheerful little company assembled, farmers on their home-bred hunters, boys on foot or on donkey-back, a few gentlefolk, a priest or two – naturally on their way to some parish call'.

She also believed that these years, when the house was regularly occupied again, was the happiest period of her father's life, 'and he made happiness around him for all, down to the humblest dependent, as he took his walks about the place, his spaniel at his heels, examining everything, greeting everyone'. The house seemed constantly to be filled with guests, much to the dismay of his wife who, 'conscious in those years of various household deficiencies as well as of the need for economy, would sometimes be moved to protest at his freely scattered invitations to lunch, to tea and tennis, even to dine and stay the night'. Inevitably, Lord Desart became involved in Irish politics, although as his daughter observed, like other men of the same class he 'felt profoundly Irish and intensely English, both at once, and could not for a moment contemplate the surrender of either allegiance'.

He was at Desart Court at the time of the Easter 1916 Rising, news of which reached him while he was playing golf in Kilkenny with a house guest, John Bernard, Archbishop of Dublin. The following year he participated, as a Southern Unionist delegate, in the Irish Convention while it sought without success to find a way of satisfying Irish demands for independence without the country leaving the British Empire. In the aftermath of this venture's failure, and the conclusion of the First World War, came the onset of the War of Independence, during which Desart Court remained untouched. A young neighbour suggested to Lord Desart 'that if he wished to send (as my own family had done) some portraits to England, I would gladly travel with them on one of my return journeys from leave, but he replied that they must take their chance'. And the chances looked good. After all, the family were well regarded locally, so much indeed that Lord Desart's younger brother, Otway Cuffe, who was both a loyalist and the president of the local branch of the Gaelic League, had been elected Mayor of Kilkenny in 1907, and again the following year. And the dowager countess, widow of the fourth earl, continued to do much to improve the circumstances of those living in the area; she had, after all, paid for the building of the Aut Even hospital in 1915. However, with the onset of the Civil War, the atmosphere changed, and it may well have been the dowager's acceptance of a seat in the first Senate that sealed Desart Court's fate, as the anti-Treaty forces engaged in a campaign of arson on the homes of senators: they could, as was suggested at the time, have mistaken the house for her property.

Looking back to the time when, as a young woman, she would go out hunting in Kilkenny, Sybil Lubbock found it hard to reconcile the destruction of her family home with the world she remembered: 'With all that friendly gaiety, could there really be ill-feeling, I used to wonder, between either the races or the classes represented there?' She felt confident that the burning of Desart Court had not been done by any of the local population, while at the same time noting 'neither did they try to prevent it'. And her mother, Lady Desart, thought that the estate's tenants 'were not above some looting and damaging of the dying house'.

On the night of 22 February 1923 a group of armed men arrived at Desart Court and, as happened elsewhere, gave everyone on the property notice to gather what they could before the place was set on fire. The family were in London, but one of the servants, Bertha Lomax, took charge and rescued as much as possible before the flames took over the building. 'She never lost her head,' Sybil Lubbock wrote, 'or her courage; as soon as the raiders were gone she saved everything she could.' But since Lord Desart had not followed the example of other house owners and removed important items of furniture and paintings from the house, a great deal was lost forever, not least the two superlative carved mahogany staircases so lovingly described by Thomas Sadleir and Page Dickinson just eight years earlier. There were valuable portraits by the likes of Zoffany and Kneller, chimney pieces of marble, those elaborate rococo plaster ceilings, and much fine furniture including a set of six mid-eighteenth-century Chinese Chippendale chairs and a superlative late-seventeenth-century Dutch inlaid walnut cabinet.

On hearing of the destruction, Lord Desart hurried back to Ireland and on arrival found a small number of objects carefully laid out on the lawn in front of the burnt-out house. 'Everything of value,' he wrote to his younger daughter's American mother-in-law, 'family history, papers, portraits, was there and has perished'. Before returning to England, he asked Bertha Lomax to send whatever she had rescued to his address in London. She duly organized for a lorry to collect the salvaged items but soon after leaving Desart Court the vehicle was stopped and maliciously set alight, so that even the few remaining mementos were lost forever.

Crushed by what had happened, Lord Desart could never bring himself to return to Ireland. 'Something broke in him when Desart was burnt,' Sybil Lubbock believed, 'something that could never be repaired.' A fortnight after the fire, he wrote to his granddaughter Iris, 'The wound is deep and there is no cure for it. Sometimes I think that I cannot bear it. The only thing is to do on and live one's life and do one's work, and be as useful as one can in other spheres of occupation.' The wound remained deep, so that more than ten years later, not long before he died, he could write again to the same granddaughter, 'I can't bear to think of Desart – it is sadness itself. All gone, all scattered – and we were so happy there.' He and his wife bought a little house in Sussex and moved there. His daughter Sybil recalled seeing him there one evening and noticing 'the look of great weariness and deep indifference that came over his face. I knew he was thinking about Desart, of the long borders in the kitchen garden and the great flowery terrace in the sunset. He could not easily become attached to a garden-plot in Sussex.' Lady Desart died in 1927, her husband surviving her for seven years. Since he had no sons, and nor had either of his brothers, the Desart title died with him.

More than a decade earlier, lacking sufficient funds and sufficient inclination, he had handed over the remains of Desart Court and its surrounding demesne to his niece, Lady Kathleen Pilkington, only child of the fourth earl from his first, unhappy marriage to Maria Preston. A claim for compensation had been lodged in April 1923, seeking £53,000 for Desart Court and its contents, together with a further £4000 for what had been lost when the lorry had been set alight. The main figure was subsequently revised downwards; in November 1924 the sum sought for loss of house and contents had dropped to £31,000. Eventually, the Irish Free State agreed to give £13,400 in cash and an additional £1200 in government stock, these amounts conditional on the house being reconstructed. Lady

Kathleen duly hired architect Richard Orpen to oversee the work and by the end of 1926 much of it had been carried out. Inevitably the interiors were much simpler than had been the originals. The two great carved staircases, for example, were not duplicated, and the house now had a single flight of stairs with plain banisters. Even so, the work went over budget and therefore in July 1927 Lady Kathleen applied to Britain's Irish Grants Committee for further assistance, explaining that her own resources were insufficient to complete the restoration. She estimated the difference between what was provided by the Free State government and what had been spent, to be £13,430, but wrote that 'I would be content to receive in compensation sufficient only to complete the house and make it habitable, say £7,000.' In the event, the following December the committee awarded her £2440.

When her stepmother, the dowager countess, died in June 1933, she left Lady Kathleen Aut Even and the other buildings at Talbot's Inch, but this inheritance was not enough to retain her engagement, and the following year the rebuilt Desart Court was offered for sale. Lady Kathleen in turn died in 1938, after which the house appears to have stood empty and unoccupied until a period during the Emergency when Irish army troops were billeted there. A contents sale was held in 1943 when all the interior fittings were stripped from the building. Five years later, the *Old Kilkenny Review* carried a report of a visit by members of its society to the house, noting that the Land Commission was 'ready to preserve the shell of Desart Court as a fine example of Georgian architecture, and to make it safe against further dilapidation, provided that some established body would take responsibility for the very small work of maintenance which would be necessary'. No such body came forward and eventually in 1957 it was demolished. Today, nothing is left to show that Desart Court once stood on this site.

10

'If the situation grows worse,
it will probably be burned down'
DERREEN, COUNTY KERRY

'PALMS, BOUGAINVILLEA, crotons, frangipani on all sides, black policemen with yellow turbans, natives of all complexions, in all manner of garb, chocolate coloured babies, with no clothes and pot bellies, dignified old gentlemen with black skins apparently walking about in their night gowns.' So wrote the fifth Marquess of Lansdowne in December 1888 soon after his arrival in India where he would spend the next five years as Britain's Viceroy. During that extraordinary period, while he was being entertained by princes and maharajas and hosting them in return at receptions and balls, attempting to keep the peace between Hindus and Muslims, seeking, like so many others before and since, to find a solution to the intractable problem of Afghanistan, spending summers in Simla and winters in Kolkata, did he ever wonder how different his life might have been had not a seventeenth-century ancestor broken a leg at the age of fourteen?

Born in Hampshire in 1623, the son of a humble clothier, William Petty, when still in his early teens, opted to go to sea and become a cabin boy on a cross-Channel vessel. After he broke his leg, however, the ship's crew abandoned him in Caen and it is indicative of Petty's pluck that he somehow managed to persuade the local Jesuit college to become a student there, while he earned money teaching English. A year later he returned to his own country and joined the Royal Navy but then moved to Holland to study chemistry and medicine and, at the same time, become personal secretary to one of the era's greatest political philosophers, Thomas Hobbes. By 1646 he was back in his own country once more and before long could be found studying medicine, this time at Oxford University where he became anatomy instructor in Brasenose College. During this period he gained fame for being one of the physicians who treated Anne Greene, a woman who had been hanged for infanticide but somehow, thanks to medical attention, survived the ordeal and lived another ten years. At the same time, polymathic Petty also managed to secure the chair of music at Gresham College in London, an indication of his breadth of interests and of his well-connected friends, both of which would continue to stand him in good stead.

By now, most men would have been content to rest on their laurels, but Petty was certainly not most men. In 1652 he secured leave of absence from his post at Oxford so that he could travel to Ireland as physician-general to Oliver Cromwell's Commonwealth army. Two years later, however, his career took another extraordinary turn. The English troops, having brutally suppressed all rebellion in Ireland, needed to be rewarded, as did the army's financial backers. The government's solution was to pay them not with money but with land, specifically with land confiscated from its defeated Irish opponents. Before this enterprise could get underway, however, a full survey of the country was required, so that the authorities knew what was available to hand out. Petty now boldly stepped forward and promised to accomplish the task in a mere thirteen months. A contract to do so was signed on Christmas Eve 1654 and the finished work duly delivered early in 1656. Because the results were set down in the form of maps, it has become known as the Down Survey.

As a reward for his labours, Petty received not just a substantial sum of money, but also his own grant of land around what is now the town of Kenmare in County Kerry. Subsequently he acquired or bought more pieces of land in the same area from soldiers who preferred to have cash, so that by the time he died, his holding in this part of the country ran to some 270,000 acres. However, quantity should not be confused with quality. When Charles Smith published his *Present and Antient State of the County of Kerry* in 1774, he described the baronies of Glanerought, Iveragh and Dunkerron, much of which was then owned by Petty's descendants, as being 'the rudest and most uncultivated tracts of the whole country'. As for Tuosist, the parish in which Derreen can be found, Smith dismissed this as 'almost one continued rock, terminated with bog'. In consequence, the area contained 'the least profitable and most irreclaimable land in the whole county'. Today, this part of Kerry is highly regarded for its inherent beauty but until the late eighteenth century, scenic charms were little esteemed: sustenance for the body was deemed of greater importance than sustenance for the soul.

Nevertheless, Petty seems to have been peculiarly attached to his Kerry property, and spent a great deal of time trying to improve it through a variety of initiatives such as iron smelting, as well as forestry and fishing. He also determinedly resisted efforts by the O'Sullivan Beare family, which from the fourteenth century onwards had been in control here, to regain lost territory. In this endeavour he won the support of Charles II who, pragmatically recognizing Petty's abilities, rewarded him in 1661 with a knighthood: Sir William, it seems, later declined a peerage, perhaps fearful of drawing too much attention to himself. On the other hand, in 1688 his wife Elizabeth Waller was created Baroness Shelburne *suo jure*. Already a widow when she had married Petty, she went on to have three children, two sons and a daughter, with him. However, in 1687, the year before his wife became a peeress, Petty died, unquestionably one of the most remarkable figures of his age.

The couple's elder son Charles, created Baron Shelburne in 1688, did not live much longer, certainly not long enough to produce an heir. Following his death nine years after that of his father, the Kerry estates passed to his younger brother Henry who became the next

Lord Shelburne (and was eventually created Earl of Shelburne in 1719); he and his wife Arabella had only one child, a daughter Anne who, although married, produced no children. So, when the earl died in 1751 his estates in both England and Ireland (then estimated to produce £16,000 a year) along with £250,000 in funds, were left almost in their entirety to a nephew, John FitzMaurice, a younger son of Lord Shelburne's sister Anne.

Anne Petty, only daughter of Sir William Petty. was described by one of her own grandchildren as 'a very ugly woman' (and Dean Swift called her 'most egregious ugly') but she was also recalled as the person who had brought into the FitzMaurice family 'whatever degree of sense may have appeared in it, or whatever wealth is likely to remain in it'. The family in question, Anglo-Norman in origin, traced its rise in this part of the country to Thomas FitzMaurice FitzThomas, created first Baron of Kerry and Lixnaw around 1260. His descendants, like so many other interlopers of the period, gradually became Gaelicized and were eventually judged to be *Hiberniores Hibernis ipsis* (more Irish than the Irish themselves). Remote from an often ineffectual government in Dublin, until the Tudor conquest of the sixteenth century successive lords Kerry happily preoccupied themselves with waging war on their neighbours. Typically, in 1325, Maurice FitzMaurice, the fourth Baron, came into dispute with Diarmaid Óg MacCarthy (from whose ancestors the FitzMaurices had originally seized land) and slew him in front of the Judge of Assize at Tralee. FitzMaurice was duly tried and attainted by the parliament in Dublin and his lands forfeited but, following his death in 1339, they were returned to his brother John, the fifth Baron.

So it continued for another couple of centuries, although the FitzMaurices and the MacCarthys eventually came to some kind of accord following the marriage of Katherine MacCarthy to the seventh Baron (who would be killed in 1410 while fighting in neighbouring County Clare). Matters grew more complicated after the death of the eleventh baron in 1541. As he had no son, the title and territory were inherited by his brother Patrick FitzMaurice, but then he died six years later, after catching cold while hunting. He left two infant sons, both of whom were dead before the end of 1549. Gerald FitzMaurice, younger brother of the eleventh and twelfth barons, in turn succeeded but died in 1550 within a month of getting married. He thus likewise left no heir.

Finally, it was the turn of Thomas FitzMaurice, fourth and final son of the tenth baron. He proved better at staying alive – and procreating – than had his immediate precursors. A professional soldier, he had spent many years on mainland Europe employed by the Holy Roman Emperor Charles V. No one knew where he was, but according to legend, his old nurse Joan Harman, accompanied by her daughter, journeyed to Milan and found him there (Mrs Harman dying soon afterwards). Thomas FitzMaurice duly arrived in Ireland, where he found a rival attempting to usurp his position. Having displaced this would-be challenger, he survived the following decades' upheavals, adroitly negotiating a path through the two Desmond Rebellions that saw the FitzGeralds, Earls of Desmond defeated and much of Munster granted to English settlers. Neither his son nor his grandson proved as skilful, and both found themselves caught up in the warfare then wracking much of Ireland. Yet somehow the FitzMaurices demonstrated an ability rare among old Irish families of the period: even if they did not thrive then at least they survived. Such was the case with Patrick FitzMaurice, nineteenth baron, who, having been raised in England, returned to that country when unrest erupted once more in Ireland in 1641; he never went back, dying in London at the start of 1661. His heir William, twentieth baron, fought on the side of James II in the Battle of the Boyne in 1690, and then went into exile to France with the defeated king, thereby risking the loss of the family estates. These were due to pass to his eldest son Thomas, who also went to France and all seemed hopeless. But in 1692, Thomas FitzMaurice returned to Ireland and made an advantageous marriage to Sir William Petty's daughter Anne, a woman who, even if not endowed with good looks, had been blessed with wealth and, as her grandson noted, sound sense. Her husband, after spending a few years in the political wilderness, was pardoned in 1700 and confirmed in possession of the family's property. Recognizing the temperature of the times, he conformed to the Established Church and to English law, for which he was rewarded in 1723 by being created first Earl of Kerry.

All of which makes him sound like a thoroughly equitable man, whereas he was notoriously hot-tempered – he once challenged the Lord Chancellor of Ireland to a duel – and, according to his grandson, more feared than loved. That grandson, William Petty-FitzMaurice, first Marquess of Lansdowne, left a frank account of Lord Kerry, describing him as someone 'who reigned, or rather tyrannised, equally over his own family and the neighbouring country as if it was his family, in the same manner as I suppose his ancestors, Lords of Kerry, had done for generations since the time of Henry II'. The earl spent most of his time at Lixnaw, County Kerry, where, his younger son John wrote, he spent 'great sums building and furnishing a very large mansion-house' along with making many other improvements in the gardens and demesne. Despite the beauty of these surroundings, his grandfather, Lord Shelburne explained, 'did not want the manners of the country nor the habits of his family to make him a tyrant. He was so by nature. He was the most severe character which can be imagined, obstinate and inflexible ... His children did not love him, but dreaded him; his servants the same.'

Inevitably, there were consequences. He had what might best be described as a tempestuous relationship with his eldest son and heir William who abandoned studies at Christ Church Oxford to join the army. There he ran up large debts before giving up his commission and becoming enmeshed in successive amatory adventures, finally marrying a woman who failed to meet with his father's approval. The first earl died in 1742 and despite the two being estranged, William inherited the FitzMaurice estates. He had little time to enjoy it, dying five years later. His heir, Francis FitzMaurice, third Earl of Kerry, was not yet seven years old and, perhaps owing to the absence of a paternal presence, perhaps due to his temperament, grew up to be a restless, lackadaisical creature apparently forever in flight from ennui. One consequence of this was that he soon fled his ancestral home, never to return. In 1768 he caused something of a scandal both within the family, and among wider Irish society, by marrying Anastasia Daly, a Roman Catholic divorcee at least twelve, and possibly even twenty years his senior. The failure of their union to receive approbation likely encouraged the couple's permanent exile from Ireland.

The Kerrys were hardly better received in England where they became notorious for their extravagance: Horace Walpole characterized the earl as a 'simple young Irish peer, who had married an elderly Irishwoman that had been divorced on his account and had wasted a vast estate in the idlest ostentation'. He bought, furnished and then sold – invariably at a loss – a series of properties in England, and commissioned architect Robert Adam to design a veritable palace, Kerry House, to be built in London's Portland Place. However, by the mid-1770s, the consequences of expenditure outstripping income were starting to be felt and the couple moved to mainland Europe, settling in Paris where they rented a number of grand houses and moved in fashionable French society: Lady Kerry became a close friend of the Princesse de Lamballe, one of Marie Antoinette's favourites. Then, with the outbreak of the French Revolution, their circumstances once again grew precarious and in October 1792 – just a month after Mme de Lamballe had been brutally murdered in the La Force prison – they were forced to flee Paris. Two of their servants, who attempted to rescue some of the Kerrys' possessions, were arrested and guillotined. The earl and countess returned to London where they were obliged to live in more straitened conditions than had hitherto been the case. She died in 1799, leaving behind a desolate husband who, on her tomb in Westminster Abbey, eulogized his late wife as 'the dearest, the most beloved, the most charming, and most faithful and affectionate companion that ever blessed man'. He then lived on quietly until his own death in 1818.

By that date, as his cousin the first Marquess of Lansdowne sadly observed, Lord Kerry had 'sold every acre of land which had been in our family since Henry the Second's time'. The immense FitzMaurice estates were gone, frittered away, and the great house and demesne at Lisnaw, where the first Earl of Kerry had once held sway, fallen into ruin. There might have ended all connections with that part of Ireland, except for the aforementioned cousin, Lord Lansdowne. His father John FitzMaurice was a younger son of the first earl and Anne Petty. Not expecting to inherit anything, as a young man he became a lawyer and then entered the Irish House of Commons representing County Kerry. However, when his uncle Henry, Earl of Shelburne, died in 1751, the property in south Kerry, that enormous quantity of land soon dismissed by Charles Smith as 'almost one continued rock, terminated with bog' was left to John FitzMaurice, on condition that he took the surname and bore the arms of Petty. This being done, a few years later John Petty was created Earl of Shelburne in the Irish peerage, and in 1760 Baron Wycombe in the English. By then he had bought Bowood, an estate in Wiltshire where his descendants continue to live.

While the greater part of his time was spent in England, the new Lord Shelburne did not neglect his Irish interests: in April 1759 he wrote to Adam Smith from Dublin expressing appreciation that the economist approved of 'my endeavours to make a part of this Country happier than I found it'. One long-term problem, dating back to the end of the previous century, was that control of the greater part of the south Kerry estate was not in the family's hands. In the late seventeenth century, during the minority of Charles Petty, his uncle and guardian Colonel James Waller had entered into an agreement with the local land agent Richard Orpen (a forebear of the artist William Orpen) leasing the property to him and another man, John Mahony of Dunloe, in return for an annual sum of £1300. Superficially, what became known as the Grand Lease appeared a convenient arrangement, sparing the young Petty heir any bother of managing his Irish lands in return for an assured income. In practice it proved disastrous, as Orpen and Mahony took full advantage of the opportunity to maximize their own yearly returns by subletting parcels of the estate, with little or no interest in what became of it thereafter.

After inheriting the family property from his childless elder brother in 1696, Henry Petty sought, with only limited success, to cancel the Grand Lease, bringing him into conflict with not just Orpen (and after his death in 1716, with Orpen's heirs) but also many of the sub-lessees who did not care to have agreements into which they had entered be subject to review. The struggle for control of the estate was continued by Henry Petty's nephew and heir, John, and then by the latter's son, William Petty, second Earl of Shelburne. Described by Benjamin Disraeli as 'the ablest and most accomplished minister of the eighteenth century', Lord Shelburne had a relatively brief but distinguished political career, holding a number of high offices not least that of Prime Minister, in which capacity he was responsible for bringing the American War of Independence to an end in 1783: for this, he was rewarded by being created first Marquess of Lansdowne. Like his father before him, he was conscious of his obligations to his Irish estates but also hampered by the continuing difficulty of regaining control of them. While the Grand Lease hindered some of his ambitions, he can take credit for laying out the town of Kenmare. Formerly a small settlement called Nedeen and located at the top of an inlet in south-west Kerry, the new town – its name a homage to Lord Shelburne's friend Valentine Browne, Earl of Kenmare, whose own estates lay further north around Killarney – was intended to represent, and to encourage, a fresh start for the estate, acting as a centre for commercial activity that would in turn lead to greater economic prosperity for the entire region.

As ever, it proved easier to regain control of some parts of the property than of others. On a visit to the area in 1770, Lord Shelburne noted that much of it was 'wild and unimproved either by Tillage, Manufactures or Arts; and abounds with Mountains and Morasses which afford a secure retreat to numbers of the Inhabitants who frequently disturb the Peace'. One such district, Glanerought, lay to the south-west of Kenmare. Representing the irredeemable landscape so disparaged by Charles Smith and other contemporary commentators, it was deemed by Shelburne's own agent Joseph Taylor to comprise 'absolutely nothing but rocks and mountains'. As noted earlier, until the upheavals of the mid-seventeenth century, this part of the country had been under the control of the O'Sullivan Beare family, the head of which carried the hereditary title Mac Finin Duibh. In William Petty's lifetime, the holder of that position, Dermot McOwen Sullivan, was permitted to live in Glanerought as a tenant. Orpen had then renewed this arrangement, Sullivan and his heirs taking possession for a term of ninety-nine years or three lives, provided they fulfilled a number of none-too-onerous conditions, one being that 'one good stone-wall house with double chimney' be constructed. This stone-wall house, described in 1777 as being in good order and with a secondary building close by, formed the core of what is now known as Derreen.

For much of the eighteenth century, successive Sullivan Mac Finin Duibhs were left to control the countryside around Glanerought largely unimpeded, no doubt assisted by the fact that there were no roads of any consequence into the district. No one, not even Lord Shelburne, ostensible owner of the property, held greater sway. In 1769, for example, Shelburne's agent sold some standing timber in Glanerought, but when the would-be purchaser went to clear the woodland, he found himself faced with '160 men armed with guns, pistols, blunderbusses and other instruments of death; besides 4 men appointed with blunderbusses to lye in ambush, to kill us on the spot if we attempted taking one Rhine off a tree'. Only after the judicious payment of bribes was he permitted to go about his work. Smuggling was a popular occupation at the time. Seemingly in 1775 a West Indian merchant vessel, *The Planter*, laden with silver and tea, arrived off the coast in a state of distress and the crew sought assistance from the local people. An illegitimate son of the then-Mac Finin Duibh offered his services and, these being accepted, skilfully ran the ship aground close to the family home, the cargo onboard quickly lost forever.

By 1763 the last of the Orpen 'three lives' had expired, in theory permitting Lord Shelburne to assume direct control over this part of his Kerry estate. Theory and practice, however, were not always aligned. Another thirteen years passed before a new Mac Finin Duibh, Sylvester Sullivan, took up residence at Derreen. He proved a very different character from his predecessors: Shelburne's agent Taylor called him 'one of the best and most respectable of your tenants'. In 1791, Sullivan paid a visit to London to see his landlord, by now Marquess of Lansdowne, who afterwards wrote, 'I am in truth very much pleased with him, and am surprised to see so amiable a character come from such an unimproved state of Society.' Appointed a Commissioner of the Peace, he was succeeded by his son, also called Sylvester and the last of the Mac Finin Duibhs. Regrettably, unlike his father, the younger Sylvester was a feckless creature, frittering away his money and falling into arrears with rent. According to the marquess's agent, his tenant was 'timid and indolent, two very bad ingredients in a man who will have to deal with the Kenmare and Tuosist people'. He died in 1809, supposedly as a result of a fall from his horse, although there were widespread rumours of foul play. On the day of his funeral the third Marquess of Lansdowne arrived in the area. He had inherited the title and estates from his elder brother, the second marquess, another restless, unhappy individual who had no children of his own and was only forty-three at the time of his death. The new Lord Lansdowne, freshly arrived in Ireland and based for a period in Kenmare, brought his wife Louisa with him and she was captivated by what they found in the vicinity of Derreen: 'It is a beautiful bay surrounded by high mountains whose broken summits make a magnificent boundary, many of them run into the bay forming bold headlands whose forms and tints vary every step you take.' In her description one perceives a fundamentally different attitude towards the landscape in this part of the country. Instead of being assessed solely in terms of agricultural potential, the region's inherent aesthetic qualities start to be considered of merit. As more visitors began to explore the area, assisted by an improvement in the quality of roads along the southern shores of Kenmare Bay, they would be as delighted as Lady Lansdowne by what they found.

Glanerought and Derreen itself, however, remained under-developed. Following the death of Sylvester Sullivan, a dispute broke out among various claimants as to who was entitled to assume the place's lease. The eventual winner was one Peter McSwiney, who in May 1815 made good his claim to live at Derreen by arriving there with a party of some eighty men and taking it by force; it also helped that his wife Lucy Browne was a niece of the deceased Sullivan. Smuggler, sportsman and duellist, McSwiney was in some respects a throwback to the roistering characters of the previous century. In 1812 he had been accused of killing a local tithe collector and went into hiding, but two years later agreed to stand trial after receiving guarantees of support from the first Earl of Bantry, who declared that he 'did not know a more excellent, or correct man' than McSwiney. The latter was then acquitted on the grounds of self-defence. Already an assistant agent on the Lansdowne estate, and a future Poor Law guardian, his right to hold the Derreen lease was soon acknowledged, but before too long the acknowledgement must have been viewed with regret. Like others before him, McSwiney began to live beyond his means, engaged in expensive litigation, took out mortgages on the property and fell behind with his rental payments. Nonetheless, his wiliness ensured it was not until 1856 that he was finally persuaded to quit the place, after being given £1200 in compensation, including the write-off of £300 in arrears.

At the time, the Lansdownes' Irish agent was William Trench, a man determined to improve the estate's management, and in consequence income, by whatever means were necessary. From the

moment of his arrival in late 1849, Trench's ruthless attitude towards
tenants, some 4600 of whom were paid to emigrate to the United
States, engendered much fear and loathing in the area, and may have
been in part responsible for what would later happen to Derreen.
That particular property, possession having been regained following
Peter McSwiney's departure, was now offered for relatively short-term
lets. Large-scale tree-planting had already taken place around this
area, increasing its appeal to sportsmen who might care to take the
place for shooting. Improvements were carried out on the house itself,
which according to the original Ordnance Survey produced in the
first half of the 1840s, was a three-storey property with outbuildings
and a walled garden, the whole site approached via a sweeping drive.
William Trench and his son Townsend Trench, who succeeded him
as agent here, were determined that in future Derreen should only be
occupied by someone they judged to be a better class of person than
had hitherto been the case. In 1857 they informed Lord Lansdowne
that the property would be 'utterly thrown away upon any common
tenant of the district' and expressed a desire that it might be taken
by some 'wealthy nobleman or gentleman who would prove a social
asset to the estate'. The first person to satisfy this qualification was
the Hon. Major Edward Bellew who not only agreed to pay an annual
rent of £100 for five years, but also to contribute to any improvements
undertaken on the property: in 1858–9 £743 was spent on Derreen,
£440 of this coming from Major Bellew. Other smart tenants followed,
among them the third Baron Clarina, his son-in-law Major Hugh
Barton and General Sir Percy Fielding, all of whom evidently met the
Trenches' exacting standards. A Mr Lovatt, on the other hand, found
his lease concluded in 1866 when Townsend Trench, who by this date
had, like several other prominent Kerry residents, become an ardent
member of the Plymouth Brethren, learnt that Derreen's tenant had not
only separated from his wife but had 'brought another lady on board
his yacht with him. Of course, such an immoral example to society
was intolerable.' The best-remembered lessee during this period was

historian James Anthony Froude who supposedly wrote much of *The English in Ireland in the Eighteenth Century* while staying at Derreen. A seat here overlooking the estuary is still known as Froude's Seat. But by the time he came to stay on the estate, it had already caught the eye, and the heart, of its owner, the fifth Marquess of Lansdowne, who, of all his family, would leave the most lasting mark on the place.

He was twenty-one and still an undergraduate at Oxford when he inherited his titles and estates. His grandfather, the third marquess, had died in 1863, but the fourth marquess only lived three years before dying in turn at the age of fifty. Prior to that, in 1864 he paid a visit to Kerry and was so much taken with Derreen that he requested additional improvements be made to the house and surrounding lands. Much new planting was undertaken on the latter, forty acres, for example, being given over to saplings of larch, fir, elm, spruce, ash and black pine. In 1865 over £900 was spent constructing an extension to the rear of the main building, as well as building a boathouse and a pier. The fourth marquess died before he could see any of the work he had commissioned reaching completion, and two further years passed before his son arrived at Derreen and recognized its exceptional character. By then, the place had been let for three years to Froude, so it was not until 1871 that the young Lord Lansdowne was able to take over Derreen and shape its gardens according to his own vision.

Small – he stood five feet six inches tall – and always impeccably turned out, Lord Lansdowne was described by one contemporary as 'possibly the greatest gentleman of his day' When his father died, he inherited not just all that land in Ireland but also the estate surrounding splendid Bowood in Wiltshire and one of the greatest private palaces in London, Lansdowne House. He also, incidentally, inherited enormous debts thanks to the extravagance of earlier generations. Reserved, hard-working, driven by a sense of public duty and the legacy of his forebears, he would hold a succession of high offices, becoming a Lord of the Treasury while barely in his mid-twenties, and then Under-Secretary of State for War. He was only thirty-eight when appointed Governor General of Canada and forty-three when invited to become Viceroy of India. In the closing years of the nineteenth century, he would be Secretary of State for War, and in the opening years of the twentieth, Secretary of State for Foreign Affairs. He was tireless and diligent, loyal and courteous, and, one suspects, just a little bit dull.

And yet, when it came to Derreen, he displayed a flair and imagination scarcely evident in the rest of his busy life. On this remote spot in the depths of County Kerry, he lavished decades of devotion: he was on his way to visit it again when he finally died in June 1927. Tellingly, his most recent biographer, and great-great-grandson, Simon Kerry, writes that it was in Derreen that he most clearly felt Lord Lansdowne's presence. Although without any of the grandiosity of his other residences, he loved the place with an elemental ferocity. His wife Emily thought he had 'an almost diseased affection' for Derreen; sometimes, after arriving there, he would lie on the grass and roll his legs in the air 'like a disembarked donkey'. Except during the years spent in Canada and India, he would try to spend at least three months annually in Kerry.

Surviving documents show how, once James Froude's lease had expired in 1871, expenditure at Derreen rose, as improvements were regularly undertaken: £678 was spent on the house and estate that year, then £794 the following year and £934 in 1873, leading Townsend Trench to observe that the property, no longer bringing in rental income, was now a 'formidable' expense, although in consequence it was 'rapidly becoming one of the most beautiful spots in Europe'. Every season more trees were planted, more rare shrubs ordered, Lord Lansdowne's desire for further improvements in the gardens being unquenchable. Its coastline washed by the warm waters of the Gulf Stream, Derreen's temperate climate permitted the introduction of species that would not have flourished elsewhere: great flocks of tree ferns, new varieties of rhododendrons, all sorts of bamboos. It became a horticultural meeting of nations in which harmony reigned supreme. Until, that is, the onset of trouble in the aftermath of the First World War.

A devoted servant of the British Empire, Lord Lansdowne had, quite naturally, been a leader of the Unionists in the House of Lords, and had strongly disagreed with the very idea of Home Rule. However, whether this was, if only in part, responsible for what occurred at Derreen from 1918 onwards is impossible to judge. In May that year a car was stolen from one of the outbuildings, but since nothing else was taken, and the door had been left unlocked, this could have been a simple case of opportunistic theft. Later that summer the river was poisoned, but nothing was done in response, owing to the 'very lawless feeling at Derreen at present and the unprotected state of the whole place and of the men who are in charge'. Over the winter months, trees began to be cut down and stolen, including eight oaks near the main house. These thefts of woodland would continue and grow worse over the next couple of years,

More sustained attacks began in April 1920 when a house in the local village of Lauragh was deliberately set alight and left gutted: owned by Lord Lansdowne (and valued at £2000), the building was in the process of conversion for use as a police barracks, making it vulnerable to attack at a time when RIC premises throughout the country were being deliberately targeted by the IRA. The following month a gamekeeper's house at Bonane, elsewhere on the estate, was set on fire and gutted, but such assaults on residential property remained rare until the following year, when the Civil War began to rage with particular ferocity throughout County Kerry. Livestock now started to be stolen: a typical note, received by the local agent William Maxwell on 30 June 1921, advised: 'Sir, We hereby commandeer three of your best bullocks as food stuffs for our army who are fighting for the freedom of your country and we consider that you should do your part in the upkeep of this army. Thanking you sincerely, Battalion Quartermaster.' Attacks on the woodland grew steadily worse, and when Maxwell went around different plantations during the first months of 1922, he found large numbers of trees either cut down or badly damaged. At Derrylough, north-east of Derreen, some 689 trees had been cut down in an area covering fifty-nine acres. 'In all cases,' he reported, 'the stump is left in the ground. In a number of cases the trees were cut leaving 2 & 3 feet high of stump standing and a number of trees left lying as they fell.' The damage was estimated to cost £670, by far the largest amount claimed for loss of woodland around the estate during spring 1922, the total value of lost trees being £1870. It would appear much of this material was put to good use in the locality: in June 1923 Éinrí Ó Frighil, Secretary at the Department of Home Affairs, told the Commissioner of the Garda Síochána that farmers and other householders throughout the area had constructed new sheds and other such buildings 'with timber stolen from woods belonging to the Marquis of Lansdowne'. According to Ó Frighil, 'there is scarcely a house in Gurtamallane that has not had new sheds built near them'. Meanwhile, the previous year, on 20 March 1922, Maxwell wrote to the IRA Cork Headquarters informing the commandant of No.5 Brigade that not only had a wide variety of items such as a donkey harness, a large landing net and two lamps been taken from one of Derreen's outbuildings, but that 'valuable plants are being taken nightly from the pleasure grounds, Chinese Rhododendrons such like which can be no use to any person'. Maxwell concluded his letter with a request that its recipient put a stop to 'this wanton destruction and thieving which is a disgrace to the district'.

In early May 1922 Lord Lansdowne, writing to his younger brother about the situation in Kerry, explained 'no rent is being paid, it is impossible to serve leases, the office was broken into and the rentals stolen some time ago … I do not expect to see Derreen again. If the situation grows worse, it will probably be burned down.' Less than a fortnight later, the main house at Derreen suffered its first break-in with an extraordinarily diverse range of goods taken from the kitchen, ranging from four large blue-patterned meat platters to six teaspoons and a reading lamp. More might have been stolen but for the fact that the elderly housekeeper Mrs Ellen Searcy who lived upstairs heard the disturbance and came down to see what was happening, causing the burglars to flee. Three days later the gardener William Arrowsmith reported that raiders had broken into an outbuilding and stolen some of its contents. On 26 May he informed Maxwell that 'yesterday the usual gang came around destroying things, brought long bamboos and thrashed all the roses off the houses', while on 12 June he wrote that large sections of fencing around fields had been torn down. Cattle were being brought onto the demesne and left to graze where they wished and, an especially defiant gesture, several dances for the local people were held in Dereen's motor house. By the summer, such incidents had become so common that Arrowsmith was able to remark: 'The usual thing yesterday, gangs of hooligans tearing things to bits, nothing more serious done.' But it was only a matter of time before something much more serious did occur.

On the night of 1 September a gang of men broke into the main house at Derreen, then occupied only by Mrs Searcy and a maid, Lily Howick. Doors and windows were smashed and a large quantity of furniture as well as blankets, linen and bedding were taken. The gardener, Arrowsmith, who lived with his wife and children close by was locked into his own house before the raid began but the following day he cycled to Kenmare and informed Maxwell what had happened. Mrs Searcy arrived in the town on 3 September, 'in a state of collapse'. On 4 September Maxwell and his wife motored to Derreen where they found 'crowds of every description round the house; men, women, and children pulling, hauling, fighting for what they could take. The house is absolutely destroyed; doors all smashed; every particle of furniture taken.' When Maxwell attempted to remonstrate, he was ignored. By this time, Derreen's cellar and its contents – including thirty-eight bottles of champagne, almost as many of whiskey and hundreds of bottles of excellent wine – had been discovered, and were in the process of being consumed. As a result, many of the raiders were soon 'lying about drunk'. Six carts were dispatched by Maxwell to salvage whatever was possible and while the main house was largely inaccessible, all of Arrowsmith's possessions and anything else found scattered around the buildings was gathered up before the convoy set off to Kenmare: on the way there, the carts were stopped in Lehid Wood and all they held was removed. However, the following day Maxwell received a note informing him that if the carts were sent back to the same place, the goods would be returned. In the event, only a few of them were, and much of what was returned had been badly damaged.

On 6 September Arrowsmith and another member of staff travelled from Kenmare to Derreen, and discovered the house 'completely gutted of all contents' and a number of men occupied with tearing up the floors. The greenhouse to the rear had been entirely smashed and rare plants lay scattered about the ground. A motor garage built of corrugated iron had entirely disappeared, as had the laundry house and a number of other outbuildings. Arrowsmith's own house was a smouldering ruin and the boathouse reduced to a shell, all its contents gone except for a motor launch too heavy to move; this had been badly damaged and its floors ripped out. On 22 September what survived of the main house was set on fire, leaving behind nothing but the walls. By this time, Derreen was described by a visitor as resembling 'the shell-swept areas of France and Belgium' in the aftermath of the First World War.

Considering what had happened to his beloved Derreen, Lansdowne, then aged seventy-seven, remained remarkably sanguine, although his son, the sixth marquess, would later write that it had been a 'bitter blow'. According to the latter, as far as his father was concerned, Derreen had been

> the 'child of his creation'. He had found it a wilderness and had made it one of the most beautiful sub-tropical gardens in Ireland. Every clearing had been made and almost every bush planted under his personal supervision. The house, originally little more

than a 'shack', had been converted by him into a pleasant if unassuming residence.

On learning what had occured, Lansdowne immediately requested that a full report be compiled of all damage to both buildings and grounds, and that his agents and solicitor submit a compensation claim. He and his wife helped to compile an inventory of house contents, the total value of these coming to £3363, four shillings and fivepence. The worth of items was often more sentimental than financial, many of them having been collected by the Lansdownes over the course of more than half a century, and quite a number being souvenirs of their time in Canada and India. There were lots of old family photographs and prints, memorabilia of holidays spent with friends on the estate, the accumulation of decades. The dining room held by far the most valuable contents, their total worth being £459 (by comparison, those in the drawing room came to £257 and the smoke room £136). Various pieces were held in particular affection, such as an oil painting of sea fish, which hung over the chimney piece in the dining room and which Lord Lansdowne remembered buying many years before at auction; although he priced this at only £35, from a letter he wrote to Maxwell in January 1924 it is clear the picture meant a great deal to him. Similarly, he remembered buying a set of antique Dutch blue-and-white tiles in a curiosity shop and although these were listed as being worth £12, he felt sure 'I could not replace them for £12 or anything like it.'

When it came to claiming compensation, a particular problem at Derreen was that although almost everything in the place had been either destroyed or stolen, quite a few items in the latter category were eventually returned. The local Catholic clergy, while they might have been politically sympathetic towards the republican movement, made it clear to parishioners that they did not approve of theft. In consequence, for many weeks afterwards, pieces of furniture, or china and glass, pictures and linens, were discreetly deposited at night either in the porch of the ruined house or else on the drive, to be discovered the following morning. Although the oil of sea fish appears to have been lost permanently, many other pictures were returned, including a set of six prints of fish by Hiroshige; it would seem these were not to the taste of whoever had taken them, since in a number of instances the glass had been broken. A valuable set of Down Survey Maps, the work which had first helped to keep Lansdowne's ancestor, Sir William Petty, in Ireland, was also recovered, again sometimes with the glass either broken or gone. Random objects reappeared, and were duly listed: among those received on 2 October 1922, for example, were a Sheraton sideboard ('damaged') and one piece of the scullery table ('sawn in two'), while those that arrived on 20 October included a circular Japanese papier-mâché tray, a water jug and four liqueur glasses. Bedlinen, a carved mantlepiece, a maple dressing table ('drawers gone'), three window shutters, even four joists: all came back to Derreen and all were recorded in a notebook kept for this purpose. The last entry is dated 18 January 1923 and lists several things such as a mahogany telescope table ('damaged') and an armchair missing its cushion. A resident caretaker, James Sullivan, scrupulously wrote to Maxwell, the agent in Kenmare, and advised what he was storing in his own cottage and what he would send on to Maxwell for safe-keeping. 'Dear Sir,' ran a typical letter despatched on 16 October 1922, 'I am sending in the mowing machine 2 chimney pices [sic] a door and a gate since their is no use in leaving anything we cant stow.' The gradual drift back of household items, with no certainty of what might turn up and when, made compiling a compensation claim for contents challenging, as did the varying condition of different articles and how much repair work they required, as is clear in a document drawn up in June 1923 that describes the various goods being stored by Sullivan.

Despite all that had happened, Lansdowne remained devoted to Derreen and keen to return there once it was safe to do so. As further evidence of the family's fondness for Ireland, in December 1922 the future sixth marquess, then still Earl of Kerry, agreed to become a member of the first Seanad Éireann (and would remain a member of that chamber until 1929, even after he had succeeded his father and taken his seat in Britain's House of Lords in 1927, meaning that for two years he simultaneously served in the national legislatures of both countries). Although the political situation in Kerry remained volatile even after the official conclusion of the Civil War, Lansdowne wanted to embark on the reconstruction of his home there as soon as possible. The original compensation claim for Derreen's contents had been £3363, four shillings and fivepence, but once various deductions were made because of returns, it was judged by a representative of the Office of Public Works to be worth £2707, four shillings and threepence. The loss of the wine cellar's contents, the damage to boats, a pony trap and so forth brought the eventual total to £4138, two shillings and twopence. But this sum was only agreed by the official in February 1924, almost eighteen months after Derreen had been left a gutted shell. Lansdowne, now aged seventy-nine and keen to see the house and grounds restored during his lifetime, found the slow process desperately frustrating. A year earlier he had written to his head agent, William Rochfort, asking to be told whether there were any further steps that might be taken to see the claim was resolved in the near future, saying 'I am anxious not to be caught napping.' Twelve months on, in January 1924, he contacted Rochfort again and suggested 'might it not be a good thing that before you leave Ireland you should call at the responsible department and point out to them that we have done everything in our power to expedite matters'.

In July 1923 Lansdowne's architect for the restoration of Derreen, Thomas Scully, who ran a successful practice based in Waterford city, had prepared a full report on what was required and what would be the costs, not just for the main house but for all the ancillary buildings: the total came to £13,855, five shillings and sixpence (£11,615 of this being for the house), plus an additional £4100 given 'the remoteness of locality'. In September Lady Lansdowne briefly visited the place with one of her daughters and was sufficiently encouraged by what she found there to report that the house and grounds could be salvaged. But the compensation claim had yet to be met and in March 1924 Lansdowne was in contact with the relevant officials in Dublin enquiring when his case might be listed so that work could begin: 'I need not dwell upon the importance of making the earliest possible start with the necessary work.' Finally, in late April, after negotiations managed by his son, agreement was reached between Derreen's owner and government officials that he should be paid £13,400 for the buildings, subject to their full reinstatement, and a further £2000 for lost furniture and other effects. The original total claim had been for £30,200, and this compromise is indicative of how keen Lansdowne was to push ahead with reconstruction of his property. As Terence Liston, State Solicitor for Kerry, gleefully wrote at the time to the Department of Finance Secretary, 'we have got much better out of the claim in respect of the furniture and other effects claimed for than if the claim were investigated in Court'.

Work quickly got underway and in June 1924 the elderly Lansdownes returned to see how matters progressed. Glad though they were to be back, as the marquess told his younger brother, the experience was in some respects a melancholy one, since 'the shells of the old RIC barracks are not enlivening – one of them just outside the gates – two fine woods which I had successfully nursed and protected are mangled past recognition – of the house at Derreen I do not dare to write'. Nevertheless, restoration work continued and by March 1925 the house was in good enough condition for the rooms to be redecorated, with the items returned after the looting of September 1922 supplemented by large quantities of furniture shipped over from England. The Lansdownes returned again that summer but it soon became evident that something was not right, and a survey on the building carried out in the autumn showed that it was it was suffering from extensive dry rot. As the sixth marquess would explain, during the renovation 'neither architect nor contractor had discovered its presence, though the walls were found to be permeated with the fatal fungus. It had thrown out its spores with extraordinary rapidity into the new and not too well seasoned wood which had been used.' His father drily remarked that it seemed to him 'as if the only real solution would be to get the house burned out again'. That option was not followed, but in order to get rid of dry rot everything had to be pulled out and all the work redone, this continuing well into 1926. It was only in the autumn of that year that the Lansdownes paid another visit to the property. He was eighty-one and it would be his last time at Derreen: as mentioned, he was on his way there the following June when he died at his daughter's house in County Tipperary. Derreen passed to his son, the sixth marquess, who shared his father's love for the house and grounds: he wrote a meticulously researched book about the history of his family's Kerry estate, *Glanerought and the Petty-Fitzmaurices*, finished just before his own death in 1936 and published posthumously a year later. His heir, the seventh marquess, would be killed in action in August 1944, aged just twenty-seven: his younger brother had died in much the same circumstances in Normandy just a week earlier. Following the two young men's deaths, while Bowood and the English estate passed to a cousin, Dereen, its demesne and surrounding woodland, were inherited by the seventh marquess's elder sister Katherine, Lady Nairne. It is her descendants who still own and cherish the property. Thanks to them, the special character of Derreen, which the fifth Marquess of Lansdowne did so much to enhance and which, a century ago, was threatened with destruction, has been preserved and can be enjoyed by visitors who are today welcomed to the site.

Select Bibliography

GENERAL

Barry, Tom. *Guerilla Days in Ireland*. Irish Press Ltd, 1949.

Bence-Jones, Mark. *Burke's Guide to Country Houses, Volume 1: Ireland*. Burke's Peerage Ltd, 1978.

Bence-Jones, Mark. *Life in the Irish Country House*. Constable, 1996.

Bence-Jones, Mark. *Twilight of the Ascendancy*. Constable, 1987.

Breen, Dan. *My Fight for Irish Freedom*. Talbot Press, 1924.

Clark, Gemma. *Everyday Violence in the Irish Civil War*. Cambridge University Press, 2014.

Dooley, Terence. *Burning the Big House*. Yale University Press, 2022.

Dooley, Terence. *The Decline of the Big House in Ireland*. Wolfhound Press, 2001.

Kee, Robert. *Ourselves Alone*. Quartet Books, 1976.

McDowell R.B *Crisis and Decline: The Fate of the Southern Unionists*. Lilliput Press, 1997.

O'Malley, Ernie. *On Another Man's Wound*. Rich & Cowan Ltd, 1936.

O'Malley, Ernie. *The Singing Flame*. Anvil Books, 1978.

Sadleir, Thomas U. and Page L. Dickinson. *Georgian Mansions in Ireland*. Ponsonby & Gibbs, 1915.

The Georgian Society Records of Eighteenth-Century Domestic Architecture and Decoration in Ireland, Volume V. Dublin University Press, 1913.

ABBREVIATIONS

National Archives of Ireland: **NAI**

National Archives, London: **TNA**

National Library of Ireland: **NLI**

Trinity College Dublin, Manuscripts Department: **TCD**

SPIDDAL HOUSE, COUNTY GALWAY

Larmour, Paul. '"The Drunken Man of Genius": William A. Scott (1871–1921)'. *Irish Architectural Review* 3, pp.28–41. Gandon Editions, 2001.

Melvin, Patrick. *Estates and Landed Society in Galway*. Edmund Burke, 2012.

Morris, Martin. *Life's Greatest Possibility*. Keagan Paul, Trench, Trubner & Co, 1892.

Morris, Martin. *Religion and Science, or The Spiritual and the Material in Life*. Dublin University Press, 1890.

Morris, Martin. *Transatlantic Traits*. Elliot Stock, 1897.

Morris Wynne, Maud Anna. *An Irishman and his Family: Lord Morris and Killanin*, John Murray, 1937.

NAI: FIN/COMP/2/7/330

Private Family Papers

BINGHAM CASTLE, COUNTY MAYO

Bingham-Daly, Theresa. *The Mayo Binghams*. Pentland Books, 1997.

McCalmont, Rose E. *Memoirs of the Binghams*. Spottiswode & Co. Ltd., 1915.

TNA: CO 762/73/6

ARDFERT, COUNTY KERRY

Clark, Mrs Godfrey (ed.). *Gleanings from an Old Portfolio: containing some correspondence between Lady Louisa Stuart and her sister Caroline, Countess of Portarlington and other friends and relations*. Privately Printed for David Douglas, 1895–8.

Keane, Michael Christopher. *The Crosbies of Cork, Kerry, Laois and Leinster*. Michael Christopher Keane, 2021.

NAI: Fin/Comp/2/8/535

Private Family Papers

DERRYQUIN, COUNTY KERRY

Bland, Christopher. *Ashes in the Wind*. Head of Zeus, 2014.

Carlisle, Nicholas. *Collections for a History of the Ancient Family of Bland*. W. Nicol, 1826.

Franklin Fuller, James. *Omniana: The Autobiography of an Irish Octogenarian*. Smith, Elder & Co., 1916.

TNA: CO 762/58/1

KILBOY, COUNTY TIPPERARY

Byrne, Teresa. *The burning of Kilboy House, Nenagh, County Tipperary, 2 August 1922*. Unpublished MA thesis, Maymooth University, 2006.

Gleeson, Betty. *Beyond the Buck Gate*. Silvermines Historical Society, 2014. https://silvermineshistoricalsociety.com/beyond-the-buck-gate.

Prittie, Henry C. *Khaki and Rifle Green*. Hutchinson & Co., 1940.

Prittie, Terence. *Through Irish Eyes: A Journalist's Memoirs*. Bachman & Turner, 1977.

NLI, Dunalley Papers, Manuscript Collection List 27, MSS 29,806-29,810

NAI: Fin/Comp/2/22/894

CAPPOQUIN, COUNTY WATERFORD

Symes, Glascott J.R.M. *Sir John Keane and Cappoquin House in time of war and revolution*. Four Courts Press, 2016.

NAI: FIN/COMP/2/23/228

Private Family Papers

BARBAVILLA AND CLONYN CASTLE, COUNTY WESTMEATH

Colnyn Castle: NAI: Fin/Comp/2/24/350

Barbavilla: TCD: IE TCD MS/11198 and TNA: CO 762/78/2

Private Family Papers

BESSBOROUGH, COUNTY KILKENNY

Brabazon Ponsonby, Vere, Earl of Bessborough. *Lady Bessborough and her Family Circle*. John Murray, 1940.

Colburn Mayne, Ethel. *A Regency Chapter: Lady Bessborough and her Friendships*. Macmillan, 1939.

Maxwell, Sir Herbert (ed). *The Creevey Papers: A Selection from the Correspondence & Diaries of the Late Thomas Creevey*. E.P. Dutton, 1904.

Ponsonby, Sir John. *The Ponsonby Family*. Medici Society, 1929.

NAI: Fin/Comp/2/10/44

Private Family Papers

DESART COURT, COUNTY KILKENNY

Cullen, Louis M. (ed.). *Retrospections of Dorothea Herbert 1770–1806*. Town House, 2004.

The Earl of Desart & Lady Sybil Lubbock. *A Page from the Past: Memories of the Earl of Desart*. Jonathan Cape, 1936.

Origo, Iris. *Images and Shadows: Part of a Life*. John Murray, 1970.

NAI: Fin/Comp/2/10/104

DERREEN, COUNTY KERRY

Bence-Jones, Mark. *The Viceroys of India*. Constable, 1982.

Everett, Nigel. *A Landlord's Garden: Derreen Demesne, County Kerry*. Haford Press, 2005.

Kerry, Simon. *Lansdowne: The Last Great Whig*. Unicorn, 2017.

Lyne, Gerard. *The Lansdowne Estate in Kerry under the Agency of William Steuart Trench, 1849-72*. Geography Publications, 2001.

The Marquis of Lansdowne. *Glanerought and the Petty-FitzMaurices*. Oxford University Press, 1937.

NAI: Fin/Comp/2/8/200

Private Family Papers

Index